Late Rally

Travel Tales, Music Memories, and Then Some

by
Stanley D. Krolick

INKWATER
PRESS

Table of Contents

Foreword

On those sleepless morphine filled nights recovering from spinal surgery, I thought about many things. My mind would wander over my earliest memories of my sick father, my mother, his caretaker, growing up in the asphalt streets of the city, the ball games, the big band music, the bookcases filled with books acquired from newspaper coupons and movie admissions and, not to be forgotten, the joys and frustrations of dating. From these scenes of an earlier life the writings emerged.

I always wanted to be a writer. The problem was I never knew it. Certainly it was not apparent from one of the earliest jobs I had. This was playing the saxophone in a five-piece band at a summer resort. The leader was Gerry Macon, a drummer. He was not that good and didn't know too much about music but he was loud and always attracted a group of admiring kids. Each night we played for dancing but Gerry's tempo was unpredictable. On Saturday nights a comedian was on the bill so Gerry had his chance to display his deafening rim shots after each gag. And I was obliged to play "Happy Days Are Here Again" as the comedian's choice of a chase. The job was easy, the pay was lousy. The best part of the job was peeking through a knothole when the waitresses were taking a shower.

At college I joined the staff of the evening session newspaper and wrote a timeless article about the school cafeteria headlined Jewish Corned Beef and Canadian Bacon. I also wrote a term paper for an English class and received a mark of B. When a classmate of mine in another English class was desperate for a term paper, I gave him mine. Not only did he receive an A plus but the piece was selected for the school magazine. The byline was not mine.

In the military stationed in Maryland I spent lots of time in the library and writing sports copy for our Detachment newspaper. Once a week I played with our softball team and the game was followed by pizza and beer at a local pub. But Charlie, our terrific center fielder who was black did not join us since this was the south and they would not serve him. Charlie was a Biologist cleared by the U. S. Government for Top Secret but could not be cleared for a beer at a pizza joint. This was a severe shock to a sensitive New York kid. I wrote about it in letters home but that was the end of it.

Out of the service, my literary pretensions began appearing and I accepted a job as a business writer for Prentice Hall. Interviewing politicians and economists was a challenge and writing up the interviews was enjoyable. My editor and I, however, didn't see eye to eye and I had to concede to his corrections even though I didn't agree to them.

Seeking a more permanent occupation I acquired a Master's Degree in Taxation from New York University and worked for several large corporations. Somehow at school I managed to sit in on a good portion of English classes. I married Barbara, raised a family, and as a sideline edited and wrote The NYU Tax Letter, a newsy Alumni publication. I took a full time job with The Journal of Taxation thinking I could write technical, legalistic, breezy style tax analyses. Was I shattered? I stopped writing for years. I had writer's block before I was a writer. It wasn't until my wife died, I retired, sold my New York residence, moved to Florida, remarried and bought a Travel Agency that the urge to restart my writings began to emerge. This was prompted to a large degree by the extensive and obsessive traveling we did.

LATE RALLY is not about baseball or the stock market. The rally I conceived was largely a literary burst of unexpected late life creative energy. Suddenly I couldn't wait to get to the computer and throw words together. They were observations or remembrances that seemed important to record. It seemed doubly important to me when faced with surgery, where risks were always looming, to get things done.

Delray Beach, Florida, June 2003

Acknowledgments

I am grateful to many contributors to LATE RALLY. Specifically I am grateful to my wife, June, who infected me with her own obsessive travelmania. Thus we both subscribed to Larry Hart's philosophy as expressed in the song "Manhattan" – "Now's the time to trust... to your wanderlust." Her astute judgment with respect to the travel pieces was usually on the money and always welcomed.

I am indebted to Marilyn and Lew of Artworx, to Barbara and Howard of Insty Prints, to the editors of Happy Times Monthly, to my brother, Bert, an invaluable fellow lecturer, and to my daughter, Jamie McGillian, for her daughterly advice. I thank Gunther Shuller for his "The Swing Era – The Development of Jazz 1930-1945," William Zinsser, Will Friedwald, George Simon, Gary Giddins, and a hundred others for the accumulation of music trivia that I absorbed over the years. I am grateful to Lisa Cohen who helped navigate me through some of the mysteries of the computer.

Introduction To "Travel" Section

After retiring to Florida, my wife, June, and I spent many months taking opera courses, walking the malls, and catching early bird dinners. The pace of this activity was not too thrilling for June. There was something missing. It came with an offer from a friend to acquire a Travel Agency. June saw this as an opportunity to utilize her extensive traveling expertise and administrative abilities. And for me, a tired accountant who had sweated out too many tax seasons, the idea of travel, or merely the word itself had an intriguing appeal.

The agency we acquired was not a full service, glamorous, mall-based Liberty Travel - like booking mill - but a cruise only, one room, two desk affair in a tiny office building sandwiched in between an animal hospital and a strip mall of auto repair shops located in far from the most attractive areas of Boca Raton. The agency had been neglected and was going downhill. In just a few years it became "Boca's best kept secret" with a faithful following that kept us unretired for eight years in spite of 911, the Norwalk virus, and the war in Iraq. We cruised as often as we could get away and cruised the world. Hence the "Travel" section reflects images of many destinations negotiated by cruise ships, a mode of travel we came to love and sell as the only way to go.

Artwork by Tony Dee

TRAVEL

Jambo

Waiting! The early morning stillness was deafening as we stood up in our stationery, open-top Land Rover, cameras click-ready, video cameras set to roll, waiting. Waiting! And trying to match the patience of two female lions sauntering slowly out of the bushes, stalking a solitary zebra, waiting as overhead vultures anticipated their share of the expected spoils.

Such are the dramas that unfold daily in the Masai Mara, the Samburu, and Amboseli that make up the National Reserve Park system of Kenya in East Africa. Jambo is the word... the universal greeting that is best defined as "I am your friend." Kenyans love visitors, especially if they are shoppers. In the shops they love to barter and they will take pens, watches, or American T shirts, and accept Kenya shillings or dollars. Having been a British colony, the people speak English. Like Sunday afternoon fans flocking to a football game, Americans have been flocking to bustling Nairobi, the jumping off point to safaris in Kenya and Tanzania. The attraction is animals in their natural habitat and photography. And for real travelers safaris are the ultimate trip: off-beat, exciting, exhausting, exhilarating and totally rewarding.

The rewards begin with game drives through the bush and extend to tent camps or plush lodges. For those heartier souls who prefer the tents, Abercrombie and Kent, a prominent tour operator distributes small battery-operated fluorescent lamps and safari hats. For June and I, as members of the more timid set, the Mt. Kenya Safari Lodge filled the bill very nicely and where gentlemen are requested to wear jacket and tie in the dining room. However the lodging one night at the Ark located in the bush was like an Army barracks and although it was spring in Kenya (October in the United States) it was rather chilly at night. I don't remember the last time I saw a hot water bottle let alone finding one at my feet under the covers. There was a viewing room looking out on a lit-up salt lick where the animals would be attracted. At 3:00 AM I heard a loud buzzer. It was the signal that an animal was at the salt lick. In this case it was a rhinoceros getting in her licks. So picture about 20 half dressed, groggy guests peering out a window at a hungry rhino. Frankly I usually reserve such nightly forays for more biological functions.

Back at Mt. Kenya Safari Lodge (the place made famous by Bill Holden) how can we forget doing laps at the pool in the shadow of snow-capped Mt. Kenya or touring the magnificent grounds at the Abedare Country Club or the stately old Norfolk Hotel in Nairobi where Theodore Roosevelt once stayed? Africa's main attraction is the animals and more specifically, the Big Five (Lion, Leopard, Cape Buffalo, Rhino, and Elephant.) These animals abound in this area as well as a generous assortment of hyenas, bushbucks, impala, cheetah, and a host of unremembered species of mammals and birds.

So there we were, June and I, in Africa, disbelieving and incredibly living life as in a dream with our driver/guide, John, who belonged to one of the 42 tribes in Kenya. We rode in a private van getting beat up on the dusty bumpy roads soaking up the sights of parading zebras and wildebeasts in single file migrating to more fertile areas. The sounds of Africa were foreign but well defined as when some elephants charting their territory honked away at an intruding buffalo.

The safari began rather uneventfully since the first game drive lasted about two hours and all we saw were a couple of monkeys swinging in the trees and some buffalo at a small watering hole. It wasn't until we flew to the Masai Mara that we saw hordes of elephants, zebra and a goodly array of impala and gazelles. There were lions hovering near a waterhole with their cubs in the early morning ready to strike for their carnivorous breakfast. We saw leopards and cheetahs in the high grass waiting to surprise, chase and claw for their daily sustenance. The surprising backdrop for all this animal action is the barren plains and the occasional acasia tree, the well-spaced symbol of the African landscape.

No trip to Africa is complete without a visit to a tribal village so off we went to the Masai Mara tribe "residence." They all spoke English particularly the wife of the Chief's son. Her name was Diana and she introduced us to each of the ladies who were decked out in their finest beads which were for sale. They are a tribe of Nomads and don't stay in one location for more than two years. Basically they are farmers and they keep their own cattle in their huts. The current market price to take a wife is eleven cows. The cattle were grazing out in the fields when we arrived but the evidence of their presence was very clear especially on the bottoms of our shoes.

Much More Africa

After seven days in safariland we needed a rest and there in the infamous port of Mombasa loomed the SILVER WIND, one of the two ships of Silverseas Cruise Line, poised for a cruise circling the Cape of Good Hope and ending in Cape Town, South Africa. We had to veritably fight our way on to the ship through the hordes of vendors. June managed to pick up a beautifully carved elephant for me to haul back home.

So we settled in to a fabulous cruise ship with only about 220 others and continued our odyssey in Africa but this time in grand style. A hearty dinner, a few drinks and introductions, a good night's sleep and we were in our first port: the exotic island city of Zanzibar in Tanzania. No Bing, no Bob, no Dorothy Lamour but miles of markets along the pier and inland. The city boasts of a former slave market and a sultan's palace and an atmosphere that seems more Indian than African. Fish was the staple and for a seafood dinner there is a choice of kingfish or baracuda. Our choice for dinner was back on the ship.

The next stop was Madagascar, the world's fourth largest island lying off the southeast coast of Africa. We docked at Nosy Be and a group of us decided to explore the island of Nosy Kumba where the brochure says "the climate is perfect" and where a rare species of monkeys called "lemurs" reside happily among French speaking natives. We had to wade ashore MacArthur-like, then fed bananas to the lemurs. Madagascar is called the "perfumed isle" because of the pungent scent of the ylang ylang blossoms.

The next port could have been named Paris and indeed Pointe Des Galets in the Reunion Islands is as French as the Can Can with expensive restaurants, Parisian street names, and densely populated inhabitants of African, Asian, and French descent. The island is volcanic, tropical, and very civilized. That night native dancers from the island entertained on the ship at a creole barbecue.

With the Indian Ocean churning up a bit, we skipped the next scheduled port and headed for Richards Bay in South Africa. We decided to get cultural and visited a Zulu village called Kwabhekithunga. The Chief greeted all twelve of our group with a vigorous handshake. Then we received a singing reception from half a dozen topless native girls, sipped Zulu beer, visited their beehive huts, and heard a traditional ceremony from a sangoma (witch doctor) and a lecture on Zulu laws against inter-marriage. We were thoroughly enthralled by it all with the whole visit choreographed by an English couple who live in the village and serve as translators and liaison with tourists.

Proceeding south we arrived at Durban, the second largest port in South Africa, the first being Cape Town. Durban's population is 80% Moslem and the city with the most Indian influence. It is sometimes called the Asian capital of Africa. We visited a huge mosque and an Indian market, passed a racetrack encircling a golf course and toured the beautiful coast lined with beaches and hotels that could have been South Beach in Miami. Vasco da Gama discovered the city in 1497 but he would never recognize it today. June toured the Valley of a Thousand Hills whose landscape ranks among the great natural wonders. The ports of East London and Port Elizabeth were more English in population with Victorian architecture and malls that resembled Main Street, USA. East London is a bustling river port handling exports of citrus fruit, mineral ore and wool with a population of 175,000. We were now ready for Cape Town.

The climax of the cruise and of our trip was just as we suspected: one of the most beautiful cities in the world. As we cruised into the harbor, we stood on the top deck amazed at the famous Table Mountain, a 3,000 foot flat-topped mountain that looks down at the city center. It is flanked by Signal Hill on one side and Lion's Head on the other. We rode the cable car to the summit of Table Mountain for a spectacular and breathtaking view of the whole Cape area. With its cosmopolitan population, museums, parks, surf beaches, wineries, upscale shops, Cape Town is truly a gem. The Waterfront Complex of shops, restaurants, African art, and South African wines is hard to beat. There's a Planet Hollywood and a Hard Rock Cafe in the city. The suburbs are smashing. We toured the wine country, lunched at the estates, tasted the wines, and literally tasted Cape Town. What a fabulous place!

And that was Africa. It was only a glimpse through a peephole but to us the so-called Dark Continent was a few shades lighter.

mv Millennium

It looked like a space capsule, sleek and shiny, as June climbed deftly into one of the MILLENNIUM'S Aqua Spa health treatments. One half hour in the capsule, we were told, is the equivalent of two to four hours of perfectly restful sleep. Once I climbed in, however, it was so relaxing I didn't want to get out. But my snoring was rocking the boat and I was forced to eject. The aqua spa, aqua gym, and the domed hydro pool were features of the largest fitness program on the high seas. It was one of the reasons June and I had to sample this 91,000 ton resort of CELEBRITY CRUISE LINE. So with a supporting cast of three other couples we set sail on a traditional seven nighter to seek out more treasures of the Eastern Caribbean.

On the third night out we voted to dine at the Olympic Restaurant, an alternative to the regular dining room fare at an additional $25 per person. We felt it was well worth the extra money. Aside from the old world ambiance and the gastronomical delights, the service was the main attraction. The courses were served to each diner at precisely the same time by a team of four waiters, each one carrying two plates. Like clockwork the plates hit the table with one single thump. And after the food was devoured or we had cried "uncle," the four waiters appeared behind each couple to remove the plates. At the given signal they reached for the empty plates, but, alas, my friend Bernie decided to reach for some scraps he had left on his plate. The team stopped in their tracks like robots, retreated and regrouped. The choreography was precise and we all held our breaths, then snickered, and finally roared with laughter, which lightened up what could have been a rather stodgy affair.

The first port of call was San Juan, Puerto Rico, always a popular spot. The ship offered trips to the rain forest, the Bacardi Rum factory, or a walking tour through old San Juan. The Dominican Republic was the next port and here, June and I were invited on a prearranged personal tour of Caso de Campo, one of the Caribbean's all inclusive gems that boasts three eighteen hole golf courses, a marina, and sports ranging from horseback riding to skeet shooting.

Broadway, Barbers, and Bernie

Back on the ship the three production shows displayed some fine vocals, dancing and costumes that were breathtaking. The "Broadway Spectacle" is always a popular favorite but we thought the "Classique" was a rare treat with a potpourri of arias

Stan and the late Harold Schein in London, 1997

ranging from The Barber of Seville's "Figaro" to Turandot's "Nessun Dorma." Other small delights on this massive frigate were a movie theatre, afternoon pizzas, daily canapes, fresh fruit, and petit fours in our suite, and a casino as regal as we've seen on any ship. There is a Fun Factory for "shipmates ages three to six" and "ensigns ages twelve to seventeen." One night after dinner Bernie and I visited the Cigar Bar called Michael's Club where we lit up a Partagas, puffed away while I was given a chess lesson from a master.

Casino, Cookies, and Cathy

Meanwhile June was rolling "sevens" at the Casino and Cathy was walking the deck to keep in shape. Norma and Bert were scouting around for their cookies and milk. Rhea and Larry were flitting between the craps and blackjack tables in their quest for a "hot table." The ever-present quizzes and trivia games were handled by the cruise staff each day. So much to do in one day we even missed Bingo!

Tale of Three Cities

Perhaps he was not thinking of Paris when T.S. Eliot proclaimed: "April is the cruelest month" — but my high school French was right on the mark when I said: "Il pleut beaucoup." So with April in Paris more like Seattle in September we set out to do the city for four days prior to a travel agent seminar in Monaco. Paris in the rain is not for tourists or travel agents. It is only for lovers and hopeless romantics. For us latent romantics, it still held a thrill.

The museums were packed and Paris was alive and gay when June and I, Larry and Rhea Herman arrived on April 11th. The crowds in Le Louvre reminded me of the subway in Times Square and getting to the Mona Lisa was more like trying to squeeze into the Seventh Avenue Express to Bronx Park. It seemed like every school in France, Germany, and Italy was let out for class trips to coordinate with our visit. Since we had allocated only half a day for this spectacular place, it was like leaving after seeing Act I of Les Miserables.

The following day we visited the Pompidou Museum and its erector-set exterior and there they were again, kids with American sneakers and jeans and NY Yankee baseball caps clowning among the Lautrecs, the Monets, the Picassos, et al. Impressionists are still the rage, as we witnessed on our visit to Musee d'Orsay, with the entire upper level devoted to more Renoir, Degas, Gauguin, et al. At the ground level was an interesting Courbet of some female body parts that was attracting some attention.

Shelter from the downpours for us continued in the Galleria Lafayette, the American Express Office, and assorted smoke-filled cafes. But we managed to view the unmatchable gardens fronting Des Invalides where the bushes and trees seemed to be marching along in unison with not a leaf out of step. There are 85,000 trees in Paris. I counted 24 in one block alone. And the chestnut trees were in blossom. One peculiar difficulty we experienced was finding a taxi driver who would take four people. It entailed clearing off the front seat of the cab which the drivers were reluctant to do. We topped off our stay with a cruise down the Seine and a walk through the streets of Montmartre in the shadows of the now folded Follies Bergere. The restaurants grew smaller since the last time we saw Paris or did we add something to our girth? We checked out of the Hotel Burgundy with four of us mashed into an elevator that accommodated at most two thin people and a couple of attache cases. The Crillon it was not. Although our location was good - in the Opera district - our room was smaller than most Holiday Inn bathrooms in the States. So much for hotel guides. But, laughing, we got to the Gare Lyon for a jaunt over the rails to the French Riviera and our next city.

Monte Carlo - Cote d' Azur

At one time the exclusive playground for the rich and famous, Monte Carlo's hotels, cafes, and restaurants bustle with tourists from all over the world and is virtually a year-round festival. And Monte Carlo is no longer considered a gambler's haven. The tourists have taken over and represent the largest percentage of revenue for the principality of Monaco. Other revenue comes from the V.A.T. (Value Added Tax). And Monaco's banking industry is second only to Switzerland in Europe. Yet the Casino is a big tourist attraction and no trip to Monte Carlo is complete without seeing it.

Monte Carlo is the largest of four districts of the principality which is nestled between the mountains and the sea and sandwiched between Italy and France. Monaco boasts of 300 days of sunshine each year. (So why did we have to come here during four of the 65 days remaining?) Monaco has 23 restaurants and many fine hotels most in the four star category. It has a population of 33,000 and an equal number who are employed there and live in the surrounding areas. It is a lush spot thanks to the hundreds of sycamores and palms which were imported by the British from more tropical areas many years ago. It is seven miles by helicopter to Nice, which is the second largest city in France after Paris.

Late Rally

We arrived in Monte Carlo and checked in at the Grand Hotel. The Grand Hotel is built on a rock adjacent to the famous Monte Carlo Casino. The hotel was formerly a Loews property now being managed by S.D.M. (Societe das Bains de Monte Carlo.) The only problem was getting to the Casino and the other hotels in the plaza. There was a giant staircase to climb and it was outdoors and it was usually raining. But the Grand is beautiful with

Stan in London, 1997

some fine restaurants, cafes, and its own casino. It is the largest hotel on the Riviera with 619 rooms.

As we checked in, the hotel was playing host to the tennis tournament following the famous Grand Prix auto race. In May there is the annual Cannes Film Festival. So this neck of the world is always exciting. As part of our seminar (the purpose of which was to sell Monaco and the Riviera as a tourist destination) we were bussed to the numerous little mountain and seaside towns like Eze and Villefranche and Cap-Ferrat. We went to Cannes (the Carlton Hotel is where the film celebrities hang out) and Nice. We hiked the twisting little streets of St. Paul de Vence, the posh suburbs of Antibes and Juan-les-Pins, names that I had read in Scott Fitzgerald's *Tender Is The Night*.

A must see is Old Town's medieval houses and the formidable Palace of Prince Ranier built as a Genovese fortress in 1215. We watched the colorful changing of the guard which takes place at 11:55 AM daily. We were wined and dined at the Hotel de Paris and the Metropole Hotel. On the last day of the seminar, the sun came out and that was the day scheduled for indoor business. C'est la vie. We boarded a bus for Genoa and the last lap of the trip.

Barcelona - Olé

After much anticipation we finally reached Barcelona, a city of cultural and architectural magnificence. Bursting with energy and life it is 4000 years old but with a young heart. It is a work in progress, a city of contrasts between old and new of cherished ancient and modern art. It is a city with a compulsion to expand culturally and economically. The enterprising spirit of the city was apparent in the challenge to host the 1992 Olympic Games. Where a 25,000 seat stadium was built for the Games, it now has been expanded to 50,000. The Olympic Village housing all of the athletes was built on the mountain of Montjuic called the Olympic Ring.

It is Antonio Gaudi's city where you can hardly go a mile without seeing one of his dazzling structures and buildings that curve unbelievably and breathe life. Barcelona also means exhibits of Picasso's cubism and Miro's modern simplicity. It is a large city with lots of fantastic things to see and yet it is a small city easy to navigate by foot, taxi or metro.

The main street is the Ramblas. It is the soul of the city that Somerset Maugham called "the most beautiful street in the world." It is a street lined with sycamores that resist pollution. There are 110,000 of them. There are a great many palm trees with shallow roots that do not interfere with underground parking and the Metro. Dinner is traditionally late in Spain. Some restaurants do not open until 10 PM.

We arrived in Barcelona on the RHAPSODY, a rather old European cruise ship that was engaged for our group of about 120 Americans as part of the Seminar. She had left Genoa stopping at ports of Naples, Malta, Tunis, Palma de Majorca, and Barcelona. The ship is not recommended. At

Naples there was a hydrofoil to take us to Capri where we were carried up to the first level of this famous rock by funicular. Malta and Tunis were uneventful. Majorca is a beautiful modern Spanish resort where we enjoyed a dinner and a respite from the RHAPSODY'S forgettable cusine. Finally Barcelona — where we arrived in the evening at the new port facility.

It seemed like the city was just waking up rather than folding its tent. There is a raised highway from the port to the center of the city which had not been completed. After enjoying another restaurant meal, we had almost a full day to explore Barcelona. And that was all Gaudi — from the exterior of the Casa Mila to the miraculous structures in the Parc Guell (pronounced Gway) with its Disneyland touch and then climaxed by the mesmerizing towers of the Sagrada Familia which has become the symbol of the city. There are four towers on the church with a plan for eight more that would represent the twelve apostles. The additional work to be done is scheduled for completion in 2060. I can only suggest: get there soon and see the four magnificent towers. I'm sure it will suffice.

California Caper

"A day without wine is a day without sunshine," as they say in the Napa Valley wine country. June and I had an abundance of wine and sunshine, as well as bowls of New England clam chowder in our ten day spurt up the coast from Los Angeles to San Francisco terminating in Lake Tahoe. We didn't do the air balloon or ride any broncos but we did drive on many harrowing roads in our Pontiac SUV up the Big Sur and the twisting 50-mile approach to Tahoe. We wound our way through S curves and hairpin curves climbing to over 7,000 feet. I get nosebleeds at sea level in Florida so you can imagine what my handkerchief looked like. June did 99% of the driving and at one point she said: "Driving over the Grimsel Pass to Zermatt in the Swiss Alps was a piece of cake compared to these roads." We skirted majestic mountain ranges on one side and deep drops looming on the other.

Hooray for Hollywood

Our tour started in Los Angeles and we elected to do an overview of the city. Although we passed on the tacky tour of stars' homes, I did insist on stopping for a photo of the Hollywood sign and a stroll along Rodeo Drive. We drove through the hot spots of Malibu and Venice where we had lunch at a seafood restaurant that June patronized when she lived in L.A. We did Santa Monica then paused

Hooray for Hollywood

in downtown L.A. at the plaza of the Performing Arts Center which reminded me of Lincoln Center in New York.

Bubba's, B & B's, and Beaches

Leaving Los Angeles, we hit Route 101, hugged the shoreline and stopped at Cambria, a tiny town that sported an array of Bed and Baths. Let me digress. B & B's are swell if you eat up that "charming" business. The small beds are usually piled high with throw pillows and cutesy touches all over the room in pinks and purples. If it has a decent shower, consider yourself lucky. Most of the bathrooms are refurbished with highly creative plumbing in old clapboard buildings that should have been condemned after the Civil War. Our reservation was at the Olalliebery Inn, not inexpensive. It oozed with charm and squeaking staircases and plumbing that was downright daring. Yet the breakfast was sensational. Although we had a private bath, it was across the hall and the flusher sounded like a rocket blasting off. We chose it because it was highly recommended by Fodors and it was at the foothills of San Simeon and the Hearst Castle.

The castle is well organized and maintained, and, after reading so much about it over the years it has been on my must see list for a long time. We toured the castle and art collection. The furnishings took a back seat to the tales of Charlie Chaplin and Cary Grant cavorting through its rooms with

assorted stars and starlets. Our guide took pleasure in retelling these stories. The dining room
with its banquet table about as long as the distance between home plate and first base had set-
tings at either end – one for Mr. Hearst and the
other for Marion Davies. The Neptune Pool was
reminiscent of a Roman Bath. The steps and staircases didn't seem to be much of a problem for Mr.
Hearst's guests. That had to be a small price to pay
for an invitation to this palatial abode.

Our next stop was Carmel, an enchanting
town with galleries galore and enough objets d'art
to fill all of Madison Avenue. It was a treat to walk
the streets with flowers and fauna in the alleys
and small shops. Our B & B had a terrace and a
fireplace and in an outrageous bow to charm, we
learned that the smooth asphalt driveway had
been repaved with cobblestones. I suspect Carmel's
residents are a bit snobbish to levy a toll of twelve
dollars just to drive along some exalted piece of
real estate called Pebble Beach. We stopped at the
Barnyard Mall for some CD's for the car. Puccini
went well with the California landscape. Carmel
was one of the highlights of our trip.

On the road again, we arrived at Monterey's
Cannery Row in John Steinbeck country and had
lunch at Bubba Gump's shrimp factory. The chowder was delicious amid all the movie memorabilia
including an actor sitting on a bench outside the
restaurant resembling Tom Hanks. We loved the
area but noted the heavy traffic around the shore.
Arriving in San Francisco we checked in at the
Wharf Inn at Fisherman's Wharf and lost no time

in having some chowder in a bowl of bread. It was dinner in Chinatown and the next day the cable car to Union Square and Macy's, ate some pretzels from a street vendor, and obtained tickets to Tony Curtis' pre-Broadway stage version of "Some Like It Hot."

It was off to the wine country. Talk about charm. Napa Valley has it. The tour was an education. After much tasting of different wines we staggered over to our B & B, the Maison Fleurie where we were greeted by Edith Piaf recordings and a house that was right out of Avignon. It was billed as "provincial charm in the wine country." The tiny bed had more springs than a Hammerstein lyric. The breakfast was expansive. There was a three pillow couch that was actually framed by a bathtub. There were old suitcases strewn about. There were old pots and pans and paddles, that seemed to come from a local junkyard. This, I imagine, gave the place a certain character. The modern fireplace was a joy in the chilly morning. The bathroom was in two parts: a toilet seat completely enclosed with its own door, and a sink and shower in an adjoining enclosure. A trip to the bathroom in the middle of the night meant negotiating three doors, flushing a toilet, and generating a cacophony of sounds that must have awakened the whole town. As Mark Twain wrote, "it had all the modern inconveniences." We thought the Napa Valley Wine Train would be a fitting climax to a short stay but it was a bit boring; merely an expensive three hour, 36 mile meal on wheels.

Then there was Lake Tahoe and modern plumbing. We checked in at Harrah's in a room with two queen size beds, three telephones, three TV's, two bathrooms, everything but a slot machine, and that wouldn't have surprised me. After a nominal deposit at the casino and a quiet night's sleep, the next day we circled the lake, a 72 mile drive of scenic wonders, a rival of any place on the planet. We made a stop at the Hyatt for lunch and an unbelievable view of the lake from the north shore. Grabbing beach chairs at the hotel's beach we basked for an hour in unbridled bliss. The sands of time finally beckoned and it was a flight back to Los Angeles for the next step in travel paradise.

South of the Border

Snuggling up with a big live fish has never been on my life's preferred agenda. Yet one of the emotional highlights of our STAR PRINCESS cruise to the Mexican Riviera was a shore excursion, June and I chose, to see what this Dolphin encounter was all about. We found it to be a rare and truly rewarding experience.

We embarked from San Pedro and headed for Puerto Vallarta, a sandy pleasure dome known for its class act sport fishing and for the Elizabeth Taylor - Richard Burton love nest. Shortly after the ship docked we jumped on a bus ready to dance with the dolphins. There were two large pools and about six dolphins with trainers ringing the sides. Four of us went into a designated area of the pool with a trainer who summoned Cherie, one of the dolphins, to play with us. We were encouraged to touch Cherie all over. She rolled over on her back. She responded gently, did some tricks, and then we each kissed her. It was totally satisfying.

There was no time left to tour the Burton lair or try our skill at the hook, line, and sinker activity. But swimming with Cherie was a large enough dose of adventure and emotion for decades to come. All I could manage was an unrestrained "wow." You wouldn't expect a "holy mackerel" would you? Until the early sixties Puerto Vallarta was a quaint village. It lies between the rugged Sierra Madre to the east and miles of sandy white beaches to the west. Today it is a popular seaside resort with tourists flocking to its water sports, horseback riding, bullfights, golf, and nature tours.

Back on the STAR PRINCESS, we greeted Pietro, Sly, Eric, and John, all of whom we had met on prior Princess cruises. Pietro, a headwaiter, advised us that "personal choice dining" was the best choice. We ate late with mostly the same table mates and it worked out well. John was a purser we knew from the SUN PRINCESS, Sly was on the cruise staff of the REGAL PRINCESS. Then we met Eric Stone, peerless pianist whom I had met when brother Bert and I did our Big Band program on the SUN PRINCESS. Eric was in rare form with a definitive version of Sondheim's "Send In The Clowns." So with all of these familiar faces on board, the atmosphere for June and I was homey.

Our tablemates were Rick, Bonnie, Dan and Rhonda. The six of us uncorked a fair share of laughs in the dining room as well as a good many wine bottles. As we ate, drank, and guffawed our way through dinner, the STAR PRINCESS set a course for Mazatlan, another popular Baja Peninsula resort. Our shore excursion was called simply "shopping, beach, lunch, and show."

The shopping in "silver country" was a town with rows of shops, most displaying silver rings, silver necklaces, silver earrings, silver goblets, and silver trinkets of all kinds and even a few shopkeepers with silver teeth. The show consisted of a Mexican dance troup and climaxed by an exhibition of the Papantla Flyers, a high flying group of dare devils who swung from a tower while we sat in an open grandstand and baked. They finally distributed bottles of water. It was either that or another Mexican War. While we still showed signs of life, they bussed us to a beach hotel for lunch featuring a variety of salads and light dishes. Then to a beach under a shady tree. We got back to the ship where it was Tequila Squeala time. That's code for nap time. Although June and I had brought along our reputations as trivia mavens, the hot Mexican sun must have done a number on us. June did manage to win a Princess sweat shirt by coming up with Princess Diana as the person who christened the ROYAL PRINCESS. That's my girl! Other than that it was total embarrassment. After another dinner of wine and roses, we considered the production show. The first one was called "Dance" and was rhythmical and a warmup for the next one called "Da Beat." It should have been called "Da Bomb." It spotlighted some energetic dancing, loud singing, and an unchained drummer. Personally, it seemed to have missed the boat... or I should say "beat." We sought relief from all this frenzy in the casino where the torture is quicker. And so to bed as the elegant STAR PRINCESS maintained her course toward the famous rocks of Cabo San Lucas.

We had only half a day in this international resort, but, we did see the crystal clear waters of the bay, the phenomenal rock formations in the harbor, a rough sandy beach, and an army of vendors. It was the day of the Asian Pacific Economic Conference and President Bush was expected, so, the town was at top level security. Wherever we turned were soldiers and rifles, a scene to which we have become strangely accustomed. June purchased her obligatory share of silver and turquoise necklaces and earrings and that completed our trip south of the border. Mexico offered sunshine and friendly people. Our home on the STAR was grand, but, Ooooh, those dolphins.

Alaska

Racing With The Salmon

June and I had successfully avoided the mere mention of ALASKA until... we browsed through a current cruise brochure which fired up some inexplicable pioneer spirit. From that point the "call of the wild" became irresistible. We were a little late for the gold rush, the fur trade, the whale kills, and the oil fields, but, the mysteries of Seward's Folly nevertheless beckoned us.

To get there we assembled a party of ten stalwarts sharing the same yen for the unexpected. We set out from our perch at West Palm Beach and hopscotched to Dallas/Fort Worth, Salt Lake City and finally Anchorage. There we saw mountains jutting into the skies with Mt. McKinley barely visible at 20,306 feet. A three hour domed train ride passing a cluster of family homes with seaplanes parked in their backyards brought us to the port of Seward. The m.v. MERCURY waited dutifully for its cargo of 1700 passengers.

The cruise started off on a casual note with a mad race to the Dining Room where early diners met head on with late diners and bedlam erupted until the smell of food soothed everyone. The first night is always rough on the dining staff but fortunately there were no casualties.

By showtime the dancers cavorted and the singers sang and the Cruise Director, Dave Cole, welcomed all to the start of a magnificent cruise. And as the MERCURY headed south toward the Hubbard Glacier in the shadow of ominous mountain peaks, partially hidden by clouds, peace and joy reigned supreme from stem to stern, from forward to aft, and from port to starboard.

Hubbard Glacier is one of Alaska's largest... stretching over 90 miles. It was formed like all glaciers when snow falls in the mountains and exceeds the amount that melts. The snow becomes a mass of ice and in time breaks loose causing a massive avalanche which flows ultimately into the sea.

As the MERCURY backed slowly toward the glacier, Pam Peterson, an Alaskan expert on board, gave an informative talk about the glaciers and the towns around them. The waters are home to many kinds of sea mammals, bald eagles, and whales. As we pointed our cameras and binoculars there was an eerie unexplainable whisper emanating from this mysterious turquoise terrain.

Rafting

The next morning we awoke in Juneau, put on the map by the gold rush, thirteen years after Alaska was bought from Russia in 1867. It has become the capital city of Alaska with modern touches but still houses its gold rush style establishments like the Red Dog Saloon.

We hopped on a bus that took us a few miles out of town to the Mendenhall Glacier. We donned ponchos, rubber boots, and life jackets and rode the rapids called "pinball alley" dodging the rocks down the Mendenhall River and getting delightfully soaked. It was one of the highlights of our trip.

A Town Called Liarsville

When gold was discovered in the Yukon, Skagway's White Pass became the jumping off point to the gold rich Canadian fields. So it was here in Liarsville we stopped to do some gold panning with a troupe of entertainers. They put on skits at a makeshift theatre in the woods called the Hippodrome. Then we were instructed on a correct way to pan gold. It was lots of laughs and as the puzzled passengers wondered how gold flecks got into their pans, the performers shouted: "because we put them there."

Blow High, Blow Low

Our trip would not have been complete if we had not seen any whales. And our quest was not in vain when we boarded a catamaran in Sitka, a city with Russian roots. Nobody, not even Ahab, hungered more for the sight of a whale than June and I. We had traveled from South Africa to San Diego but it was only here on the shores of Sitka, Alaska that our dream was fulfilled. Humpbacks and Grey whales were sighted on the starboard, the port, and the bow of the boat. We couldn't focus our cameras fast enough to catch these fantastic creatures. After a day of sighting whales, sea otters and bald eagles, we could not pass up a salmon bake at a wilderness oasis not unlike Florida's Jungle Queen in the everglades.

The final stop on the MERCURY'S odyssey was a sleepy shopping town called Ketchikan. It's long main street harbored shops cluttered with all sorts of merchandise from eskimo dolls to hunting rifles... but it's claim to fame is having the world's largest collection of Totem Poles. Other excursions in Alaska were helicopter rides, sport fishing, nature walks, bike rides, kayak experiences, and a scenic railway. All of these shore excursions were handled very efficiently by CELEBRITY.

Leaving Alaska through the Inside Passage with all its natural wonders visible on either side of the ship we headed toward Vancouver, a truly fabulous city. Together with Victoria, also a Canadian jewel it was the topping on the cake.

Hawaii

The river of white hot lava snaked slowly down Kilauea mountain sparkling, shimmering, lit up like a parade of endless torches... giving off a spectacular light show that has been going on since 1983. And from the decks of the MS STATENDAM, passengers aimed their cameras and binoculars at this beguiling and bewildering natural phenomenon. The chorus of "oohs" and "ahs" was accompanied by the night's stiff breeze.

This volcanic close-up is one of Hawaii's many tourist attractions. And tourists we were. June and I were not disappointed. With nine days at sea and six days ashore, it was an ideal mix. The STATENDAM is a nine year old ship - old by today's standards - but spruced up to look fresh and new. The typical HOLLAND AMERICA amenities were ever present - popcorn at the movies; hamburgers and hot dogs every afternoon, cloth towels in the restrooms, fresh flowers everywhere; and best of all, the amazing bread pudding daily.

That's Entertainment

We have often lauded the entertainment on HOLLAND AMERICA ships which present a healthy balance between modern musical tastes and the traditional Broadway. The STATENDAM was no exception. The first show was called "Sentimental Journey" an overview of the shows that were to follow. There was "Copacabana," the Barry Manilow opus. The final production was "Showstoppers" with dancing and singing from "Kiss Me Kate," "A Chorus Line," "West Side Story," and other perennials.

When the cast rested, there was Pearl Kaufman, a Hollywood legend, who played piano and had her musical hand in some of the best Hollywood musicals. Listen to the piano on the soundtrack of "Dr. Zhivago" or "Rocky," you'll hear Pearl. We also enjoyed Barbara Minkus, who was the original Lucy in New York's "You're a Good Man, Charlie Brown," and toured the country in "Funny Girl" as Fanny Brice. Her performance in the ship's Van Gogh Lounge brought the house down. We can't forget the guy who kept things going. No, not the Captain but Dave Shermet, the Cruise Director, one of the best we've met.

Destination Hawaii

On Hawaii we saw deserted volcanic islands, any one of which could have been Bali Hai, soaring mountain peaks that hid in the clouds; amazing waterfalls; wide sugary sand beaches that were all public; friendly taxi drivers and guides who could spout out rainfall statistics and historical data like college professors.

Hawaii consists of 132 islands in the middle of the Pacific Ocean. The M.S. STATENDAM docked at four of these islands: Hilo and Kona, which are on the island of Hawaii, otherwise known as the Big Island; Oahu, the most populated, with Honolulu, the capital city; and the magnificent Waikiki Beach; Maui with its port cities of Lahaina and Kanapali; and Kauai, the garden isle where movies are made like "South Pacific," "The Thorn Birds," and "Jurassic Park."

HILO

Hilo was our first port of call and the reception was fitting with hula dancers and a Hawaiian band. It's a gloomy island averaging about 130 inches of rainfall each year. Hilo's attractions are its black sand beach, tropical rainforest, and volcanoes. Kilauea is the world's most active volcano. The molten lava can be viewed from a helicopter but I preferred to view the nightly flow from the comfort of a ship's deck chair.

Hilo is also noted for its flowers (mainly orchids), papaya, and macadamia nuts. And no visit to Hilo is complete without a stop at Hilo Hattie's – the Hawaiian store. There is a large selection of gifts, souvenirs, foods and fashions and the best price for the 4.5 oz. cans of Mauna Loa Macadamia Nuts. We had a carton of goodies mailed home.

OAHU

The next port was Honolulu and world famous Waikiki Beach. Honolulu is the commercial and financial heart of the State. Within its cosmopolitan characteristics it boasts of sugar cane fields, jagged cliffs, mountains that rise to 4000 feet and dormant volcanoes. Our first stop Pearl Harbor and while we expected a two to three hour wait, we breezed in probably because there was only one ship in town. The Arizona Memorial is moving and sobering. The atmosphere is solemn; the movie shown at the memorial includes actual footage taken by the Japanese during the December 7th attack. We drove back to Waikiki nestled in the shadow of the Diamondhead stopping first at the Hyatt Regency then at the Hilton Hotel and Hilton Hawaiian Village. At a bar on the beach, June had a Tropical Itch, I had some bikinis in my sights. We passed the Iolani Palace, once the home of Kings and Queens and is the only royal palace on United States soil... excluding Trump Tower, of course. On our must-see list was the famous Royal Hawaiian Hotel (built in 1927) where we arrived too late for a luau. Ah shucks! Instead we dined at the Sheraton on the beach and were entertained by hula dancers and singers until night fell. And then it was back to the ship for more dining, drinking, shows and blackjack.

MAUI

The island of Maui was next. The town of Lahaina, once a whaling village, has become a hot tourist spot. The Tahitians lived here around 800 A.D. In 1778 Captain Cook paid a visit to the island which had become the whaling capital of the world. In winter humpback whales migrate to the waters of Maui. Kanalapi Beach has a whaler museum and Whaler's Village is an upscale shopping area with a flurry of fine restaurants along the beach. The Sugar Cane Train chugs along from Lahaina to Kanalapi through fields of sugar cane. It is an open sided 1890 style train with wooden cars built in England in 1888. The route passes through a row of grand hotels. June went to see the Hyatt Regency while I preferred the breezes on the beach.

KAUAI

Nawiliwili is the main port on the island of Kauai. It is a lush island with green landscapes and a variety of plant and wildlife, dramatic canyons and pristine beaches. It is often called Hollywood's paradise and is the location of choice when the script calls for blue Hawaii.

Late Rally

Given the time restraints of only one day in each port, we saw enough of Hawaii to absorb the energy and appeal of the 50th State.

Down Under

Albatross colonies, penal colonies, hot pools, mud pools, Maoris, Aborigines — all legends of Australia and New Zealand. They became reality for June and I when we boarded ROYAL CARIBBEAN'S LEGEND OF THE SEAS for a 14 day cruise from Auckland to Sydney.

The action began in Auckland before we boarded the ship. We were joined by Florida friends, Dale and Jerry Lieberman. After the long flight from Los Angeles, we checked into the Hyatt Regency and virtually collapsed for a few hours. The usual tour bus overview of the city was followed by a harborside fish dinner. An after dinner stroll back to the hotel seemed like a good idea, at the time, since our map of the city showed the distance to be a few short blocks. However, the map didn't show altitude and the hike was in one direction – up. There were four sore backs that night.

The next day we boarded the LEGEND OF THE SEAS. It was the time of the America's Cup regatta and the city and the harbor were all aglow with horns & excitement everywhere.

Team New Zealand was defending the Cup it had won in 2000.

The City of Sails

New Zealand is a small country consisting of two islands, north and south. Auckland in the North is the most populated city in the country. The city's balmy climate is a natural for boating and "there are more boats per capita than any other city in the world," according to the tour books. Enhancing the city's cosmopolitan flavor are a large Maori community and immigrants from various countries.

June and Dale lost no time in exploring the town and went off to Sky City and the observatory tower the tallest free standing structure in the Southern Hemisphere. It has choice restaurants, two casinos, and an amazing view of the city. On the ship, we met Bill Brunkhorst, the Cruise Director, from New Jersey, an affable former dancer, who has been a Cruise Director on many of the Royal Caribbean ships since 1988. We sailed for our first port of call which was Tauranga, the gateway to Rotorua noted for its kiwi fruit, Maori craft village and museum, and its startling thermal activity.

We rented a van with driver to get us to Rotorua, a one and a half hour drive, and were accompanied by two other couples from our dining room table. Rich and Beth were from California by way of New Jersey and their friends, Dr. Gerry York and his wife, Marlene, hailed from Reno. Our group jelled immediately. Rich and Jerry made with the jokes and Rich and Marlene traded friendly barbs. At a town called Te Puke we were in the kiwi fruit Capital of the world touring the fields of this furry fruit in a cute little trolley train in the shape of a kiwi. We were rewarded with samples at the end of the tour.

We proceeded to the Maori Arts and Crafts Institute, a cultural show and a photo shoot of native Maori men and women with painted faces, arms and backs. We could only imagine how the other parts of their bodies were painted. From there we toured the thermal reserve known as Te Wharaewarewa, an incredible display of boiling mud and geysers. On the drive back to the LEGEND we passed Mount Maunganui, a popular beach resort and shopping area not unlike Malibu or Fort Lauderdale. In the dining room, Jerry and Rich, our Bocaccio boys, again matched jokes, and the duel would continue until the end of the cruise.

Sheepdogs and Fire Chiefs

The next port was Christchurch, the most English of New Zealand cities with its lush gardens, parks, and Gothic buildings. Driving out to the countryside we set our sites on Manderley Farm where we watched sheep being sheared. But much more fascinating were the sheep dogs herding the sheep down from the mountain. We were astonished to see the discipline of these miraculous dogs.

Continuing on the picturesque road to Akaroa we stopped for an outdoor lunch at the French

Farm Winery located on the crest of a hill with wonderful views of the sea and the mountains.

If Christchurch had an English heritage and Akaroa decidedly French, Dunedin owed its prosperity to the Scotch. While a large number of the citizens of New Zealand had ancestors from the penal colonies, the Scotch came to New Zealand for religious freedom and they came not as paupers. They built fine houses with exceptional architecture and developed a thriving community. It certainly didn't hurt them when gold was discovered in the Otago Hills. We drove through the city and then onward to Fort Taiaroa with a view of the "disappearing gun" installed in the 19th century to ward off a possible attack from Tsarist Russia.

The Albatross and The Penguins

We were not prepared for the next activity which brought us to the brink of another uphill trauma. It was a visit to the famous albatross colony. The albatross is one of the world's largest birds with a wingspan of up to ten feet. To observe these special creatures in their natural habitat, there were a number of steep hills to climb. It seemed endless... but how could one visit New Zealand without a peek at this flying phenomenon, the 747 of Bird Land? When a guide saw me gasping for air, she set me up in a motorized scooter and June and Dale held on to the back of the seat as we rode up to the observation post. Many laughs but there was more to come.

Our wildlife explorations reached a climax with a safari to the yellow eyed penguin reserve. This was a rare opportunity to photograph at close range. These penguins choose to breed in a very private place and they are constantly threatened by predators. Was it our destiny to try to save these pitiful birds? So onward we trudged down from a mountain top through a series of narrow tunnels of dirt, single file, Viet Cong style, and ever fearful of talking which would scare these perishable creatures. Finally we were able to see four tiny ones in a heap of grass and gingerly snapped our photos. Each one was about the size of a football and if my legs were what they once were, I would have kicked them right through the roof of the tunnel and into the sea. Since it had cost $28 for the tour, the bottom line was $7 per penguin. Thus our contribution to conservation was inscribed. I hate to even mention the upward climb back up the mountain (without a mobilized chair.) The whole thing was underwhelming, but at the time there were heaves of hilarity.

The next day at sea we were able to relax on the top deck while the ship snaked its way through the magnificent Milford Sound, Dusky Sound, and Doubtful Sound. With mountains and waterfalls on either side of the ship, these natural wonders of the Fiord National Parkland attracted a maze of camera activity. That night was the first production show on the ship, a ditty called "Make Mine Broadway" which wasn't too hard to take. Another night was the familiar comic, Marty Allen and his wife, Karen, who put on an excellent show.

Sleepy, Historical Hobart

Under the shadow of Mount Wellington, Hobart is a small unspoiled bastion of the English lifestyle on the island of Tasmania. We visited the Richmond jail which dated back to the early 1800's. Here we saw the solitary confinement cells and "heavy irons."It was an interesting photo shoot but nobody was interested in trying on the leg irons for the camera.

The next stop on our tour was the Wildlife Park where we were suddenly met by an onslaught of flies. That's when we learned the Australian salute, by waving away the blasted insects. Finally we parked at a shopping street where June purchased a cute little clock made from the wood of the Sasafras tree. It looks great on our shelf but I am still trying to figure out how to set it. So much for Hobart.

Wineries, Wildlife, and Puffing Billy

We sailed for Melbourne, Australia's cultural capital, with its galleries, museums, theatre and opera where the tour books say "culture is celebrated with unrivalled gusto." There are a variety of restaurants and festivals galore from film to fashion to food and comedy. With all of this interesting stuff, our sophisticated city group voted to see the countryside, the Yarra Valley, and the Dandenong Range.

Another mistake was hiring a van with a driver who had never been outside the city center of Melbourne. But our June took him in tow and with detailed map navigated us through the wine country and some breathtaking scenery. One of the more interesting segments was boarding the Puffing Billy train for a few miles with a gang of school kids on a field trip with legs dangling from the side of the train. So we got into the swing of things and we all dangled.

We stopped at a winery for lunch and a wine tasting in the Yarra Valley. Heading back through the city of Melbourne and then to the ship we prepared for what was to be a rousing Valentine's Day dinner. Marlene bought Rich, a pair of red undershorts for Valentine's Day. On a dare from Rich, Marlene climbed up on the table and then with Rich putting on his undershorts he climbed up on the table. The dining room went wild. The professional comedy show that night ran a poor second to the laughs in the dining room. Marlene became as notorious as the Dixie Chicks.

The City of Sydney

In our travels we've witnessed many inspiring scenes like sailing into New York Harbor past the Statue of Liberty; peering up at the Statue of David in Florence; gazing in awe at the embarrassment of riches in St. Petersburg's Hermitage; breathing the air of the Author's Lounge at the Mandarin Oriental in Bangkok, and viewing the last act of Turandot. Adding to these dramatic sensations was the early morning eye-opening sight of the Opera House from our balcony as we cruised into Sydney harbor and glided slowly under the Sydney Harbor Bridge.

Like many of the world's major cities, Sydney is a contrast of old and new. There are soaring glass and steel skyscrapers offset by old historical buildings. Where Captain Arthur Phillips' 1,000 convicts from England set foot in 1787, today is a beautifully restored area called The Rocks. A few minutes away is the 48 story Australia Square Tower where the entire city can be surveyed. The sights include Darling Harbor, the Monorail, the Maritime Museums, Chinatown, mimes all around, shops of all kinds... and tourists. Amid the shops and tourists at the Queen Victoria Building June and I had an earful of the Didgeridoo, a long wooden instrument that is used for Aboriginal ceremonies.

The Harbor Bridge was built in 1932 and can be climbed to the summit 400 feet above the sea. It's billed as "the climb of your life." We took the much safer four hour harbor cruise with a tasty lunch on a sunny day passing quaint little beaches, amusement parks, and boats of every size and shape in the harbor. From almost anywhere in the harbor the Opera House is visible and stands as a symbol of Sydney's status in arts and architecture. It took 15 years and 102 million dollars to build.

We explored The Rocks where a gigantic flea market is held each weekend. There was a jazz band marching up and down the street like something out of Bourbon Street. June and I sat for a sketch by a Japanese artist. We munched on a bag of goodies and ogled at the assortment of Opals.

That night we dined on the sands of Watsons Bay just a few feet from the shore at a place called Doyles. The next day we bussed to Manly Beach comparable to any of the South Florida spots, and our choice over the more popular Bondi Beach. We spent about two hours at the Holocaust Museum. We drove through Blue Mountain on the outskirts of Sydney then on to Featherdale Wildlife Park. We snuggled up to the Koalas for photos and fed the Kangaroos and sneered back at the Tasmanian Devils. We toured the Olympic Village the site of the 2000 Olympics. At the Intercontinental Hotel we had a light dinner and were ready for the trip home. We needed another month to see Australia's Outback, Ayres Rock, and the Great Barrier Reef. But, another time.

Panama

In 1996 we cruised on the SUN PRINCESS shortly after its inaugural. The ship was the first of a new wave of PRINCESS ships. Judging from this ten day sailing to the Panama Canal, she hasn't lost her lustre. And neither has she lost her superb Maitre d' Mr. Giorgio Pisano. He keeps his chefs and staff going full blast with two main dining rooms, personal choice and traditional, early and late dining, alternative dining at the Sterling Steak House, Verdi's Trattoria or the 24-hour Horizon Court. And lest we forget (and I didn't) the franks and burgers on the Terrace Grill each day. As the comedians say, "you come aboard as passengers and leave as cargo."

But food, of course, is only part of the SUN story. She has added internet and e-mail service at the Business office. There were four computers and they could have used eight. I was a steady customer, hip hopping from there to the gym to the aft pool daily. This cruise to Panama was packed to the rafters as most of the PRINCESS ships are in this post 911 travel binge.

I was on the ship with brother, Bert, since we were selected to do our Big Band music lecture series. We did the World War II songs; a Sinatra program; big band vocalists; and finally tunes from America's best composers. We gave them music, quizzes, prizes, and big band trivia. What more could a person over 60 desire? For one fleeting moment we were back in the fabulous forties. The excitement was electric. There was dancing in the aisles and it was the best of times.

Combos, Comedians, and a Canal

The other entertainment on the ship was of the usual professional calibre. The first production show called "Words and Music" featured a cluster of fine show numbers and dazzling dancers. There were combos, comedians, and singers, filling all the lounges with gaiety. Art auctions, Bingo sessions, Bridge instruction were other leisurely options all brought together by Cruise Director, Simon Weston.

Passengers chose this cruise to see America's miraculous engineering feat and the voyage certainly offered loads of information about the canal. We learned from a Panama Commission commentary about the first ship to traverse the canal in 1914, the largest ship, the smallest ship, as well as the astounding individual who swam the canal in 1928. That's one for the trivia mavens.*

Richard Halliburton who paid a toll of 36 cents.

The Far East I –
Beijing To Bangkok

After an arduous flight the four of us (June and I, Bernie and Cathy Lipsky) were met at Beijing's airport by Norman, who was our guide for the four-day stay in China's capital city. We were driven by van to the Grand Hotel where it required five clerks and 45 minutes to check us into our suites. The city is a sprawling mass of high risers. The streets are jammed with bicycles and pollution is rampant.

The hotel was, indeed, grand with an atrium view of the main floor decked out in red and gold, trimmed with ornate statuary, and a grand piano in the center of the main floor. So, looking down from our fifth floor landing and listening to a classical pianist who alternated with a chamber music group dressed in formal attire was an elegant sight. The atrium was large, the rooms were large and everything about China is large.

Everything, that is, except Norman. He was a short, young vibrant student type who knew his Chinese history and was not shy about spitting out dates and emperors' names in excellent

English. (And we in turn taught him some choice American idioms.) On the first day, it was a bit nippy and we hopped into the van for a short drive to Tiananmen Square, the largest square in the world. We recalled the 1989 demonstrations, and Chairman Mao's tomb, and seeing these images on TV screens only ten years ago. There were Chinese soldiers and policemen scattered about the square. What seemed odd to me was their shabby and ill fitting uniforms. Some of them even wore sneakers.

This was the jumping off point to the Forbidden City which was a series of temples, pagodas, steps of all sizes and shapes, vast courtyards, with swarms of people and a persistent arctic wind that we didn't expect and were not prepared for. What we hadnrealized was that the Forbidden City was not just a few blocks behind

June at the Forbidden City, Beijing

a huge facade. It just went on and on and Norman kept up his history lesson as we entered the Temple of Heaven, the Llama Temple and a score of others as if we could absorb all the dynasties and emperors about which he spoke. The day was exhausting and I declared my farewell to climbing any further steps. Dinner that night was at a family-style restaurant that was not sensational (chopsticks optional.)

Day Two was a bit more varied. We had a brief rickshaw ride through a modest Beijing neighborhood and a visit to a schoolhouse where June had a ball showing the children her digital camera. Norman took us to a typical Chinese family residence which was rather cozy. Judging from all the laundry hanging out from the buildings, the Chinese either don't believe in dryers or General Electric has not yet arrived. Then we visited an ancient Chinese Prince's mansion and gardens and to Silk Alley for T shirts, cheap watches, and silk ties, and to a Cloisonne factory. Then it was off to the Summer Palace, a lovely cruise on the lake and lunch. This was also a family-type restaurant with undistinguished food although my companions were a lot more tolerant than I of Beijing cuisine.

That night we saw the Beijing Opera which was a far cry from the Metropolitan. All I remember were the screeching sounds and swords swishing back and forth. When we got out of the theatre we were looking for a place to have a cup of coffee. Thank God for McDonalds. With the coffee I even threw in some fries and a burger and all was right with my world.

The next day started out with a visit to a jade factory, a very classy establishment where the display was enormous. There was jade of every size, shape, and color and where it was stressed that "gold may be precious but jade is priceless." From there it was the Friendship Store, a government owned department store that sold a variety of wares, but not exactly a Bloomingdales. Dinner was of the same type: family style, middle class fare. I think at this point we hungered for one of the better rated restaurants but we were committed to Norman and his tour schedule. Well the final day promised a lot more. We were to visit the Great Wall and dinner at a Peking Duck restaurant. We drove to Bedaling. The wind had not subsided and I am indebted to Bernie's extra wind breaker which came with a hood and a pair of gloves. The sight of the wall after being taken up in a cable car is awe inspiring. The mountains and the length of this twisting pile of rocks is breathtaking. It was truly the highlight of our four day sojourn in Beijing. The Peking duck that we thought would finally be exceptional was not.

At dawn, Norman and his van picked us up for the hour and a half drive to Xingang where we boarded the SKY PRINCESS. Norman's eyes almost left their sockets when he saw this elegant ship. Here was a young man who had never left Beijing and I don't think he had ever seen anything as luxurious. He had no desire to see the United States or to travel anywhere but content to spout out the Chinese history about which he was so proud. We said goodbye to Norman.

Shanghai

We arrived in Shanghai the largest city in China and with its twelve million residents one of the most densely populated areas in the world. With a decent port, an inexhaustible labor pool, and western technology, Shanghai became China's most cosmopolitan and most westernized city. We took a shuttle bus from the ship to a Friendship Store, where we engaged a taxi whose driver didn't speak or understand English. However we had gotten written instructions in Chinese and a map of the city so that we were able to communicate and visit some tourist spots. These included a pleasant drive through downtown passing old stone buildings along the harbor known as the Bund and Nanjing Road, the Fifth Avenue of Shanghai. The overview continued with a stop at a children's palace, formerly a mansion of a Shanghai millionaire, which was now a huge school. We then drove to the sixteenth century Yu Gardens, built by one of the Ming Dynasty's rulers. Its flowers and structures represented a sampling of landscape art out of China's past.

Since we were in the heart of Old Town with its narrow alleys we resumed our exploration by foot amidst an array of street scents ranging from fried dim sum to spices, perfumes, and tobacco. The bargaining over knickknacks was right out of basic flea market but such negotiations are expected. As June says, "never be embarrassed over a bargain."

Back on the ship at sailaway time, the buildings lining the edge of the harbor were all aglow. Just the thought of having been in a legendary place like Shanghai brought to my mind images of mystery, intrigue, and Orson Welles' movies. We slowly set sail for Hong Kong.

The word from Hong Kong — Shopping

The SKY PRINCESS cruised into lit up Hong Kong harbor at 6 AM on Day 8 of our journey – spectacular sight of harbor dotted by massive skyscrapers – We joined tour group for overview of city – Guide on bus was Fred native of Hong Kong grey slacks and blue jacket – affable fellow full of Hong Kong information – only 35 minutes from mainland China – 6.5 million residents but probably more with many illegals – saw site of proposed Disney Park – Bus climbed to Victoria Peak – Fred pointed out homes of Chinese millionaires somewhat like a Rich and Famous show – Fred proud Beijing changed nothing after takeover from British – Some apartments on Peak rent for $25,000 a month – Out of bus for photos from Peak and visits to bathrooms that Fred called "happy rooms" – crowds straining for best views – Back on bus bound for Aberdeen and fun Sampan cruise – Boat driven by middle aged Chinese women – some

families still live on junks – snapped many photos
– Fred rounded up people for drive to Stanley Market and mini shopping spree – Low prices on luggage, silk ties, T shirts – lots of people – Back on the bus for ride to Nathan Road upscale shopping area – We left tour for walk through colorful streets – all kinds of shops – many camera, eyeglass stores, and restaurants – Stopped for lunch – buffet style – Better than food in Beijing – Walked off meal through streets of Hong Kong with sounds of jackhammers and construction on every corner – hordes of people.

Good Morning, Vietnam

Our first sight of Vietnam was the lively port city of Nha Trang. Nestled in the green hills of South Vietnam, it is noted for its fishing industry and is also a popular beach resort. As we left the port on our tour bus with an excitable guide named Hai, we passed coco palms and tree-lined sandy beaches that reminded me of Puerto Rico. The bus threaded through the downtown area of small one story shops and cafes and bicycle clogged streets.

There were backyard farms where bananas and coconuts grew, and water buffalo and rice paddy fields as we drove into the countryside. We stopped at a farmhouse in a rural area where the people were happy to see us. At a country cafe Vietnamese dancers and musicians played for us in traditional dress. They served us fruit drinks sipped from a coconut shell. There was a straw factory where straw mats were made. When we visited a bread factory with ovens going, it was a bit too hot to linger but the bread was tasty. At every stop there were children of all ages, some barefooted, selling post cards, T shirts, and the traditional cone-shaped straw hats.

Enroute back to the ship, we got out to view the harbor and fishing boats and stood on a bridge that had been bombed out during the war and rebuilt. Nha Trang was once the center of an ancient kingdom where its hilltop is still regarded as a holy place. We'll remember it as a place where gentle people lived who were obviously pawns in a nasty war.

Saigon or Ho Chi Minh City

Ho Chi Minh city better known as Saigon, has an international flavor where cars and motor bikes swell the streets and wide boulevards, where the

Beating the heat in Vietnam

sounds of hawkers mingle with the honking horns and the purr of the motor bikes. It is a city where French colonialists developed a swampland into a leading Asian metropolis. We visited the famous Rex and Caravelle hotels from where reporters filed their stories on the progress of the war 25 years ago. It is also a city of friendly faces and charming shops. Unfortunately, our guide was not too helpful in pointing out the places to be noted referring to the city as Ho Chi Minh and never mentioning Saigon or the many French structures like the Notre Dame Cathedral. He never mentioned any French influence at all. But the tour bus did let us off at Reunification Hall, the former Presidential Palace. Another stop was the Water Puppet Theater located in the History Museum. This is a unique Vietnamese art form.

Sadly, we left Saigon but glad that we had seen a country recovering from devastation and a civil war that claimed so many casualties.

Scintillating Singapore

Within this modern metropolis of glass and steel high risers are Buddhist temples, Arabian bazaars, and one of the busiest harbors in the world. As we pulled into the dock laced with towering buildings, it could have been Wall Street, U.S.A. Diversity is apparent among the three million people who inhabit Singapore, an independent country. The four main languages are Malay, English, Chinese, and Tamil. The major religions are Buddhism, Taoism, Islam, Hinduism, and

Christianity. English is taught in the schools and the English colonial era lingers on with cricket matches every weekend and some of the finest hotels in the world.

Modern Singapore dates back to 1819, when the popular Sir Stamford Raffles arrived and persuaded the Sultan to cede Singapore to the East India Co. Raffles was an enlightened administrator and his lasting monument is the world famous Raffles Hotel. We toured the lobby, snapped a few pictures, stopped at the Botanic Gardens ablaze with orchids, and then to Little India. After some curry tasting and spirited touring in this colorful area, we proceeded to the Fifth Avenue of Singapore – Orchard Road – a collection of some of the most exclusive retailers in the world.

As time was running out we ambled into the Galleria Mall which sported more designer names than a Parisian fashion show. Although we didn't get around to much of the city, we did get a feel for this unique part of Southeast Asia, the link between China and India. One thing we learned in Singapore: one who litters can end up with a jail term.

Bangkok – The Venice of the East

The end of our cruise and the climax of our journey was Thailand, a country never subjected to colonial rule by a Western nation. Proud and independent Thais call it "the land of the free." Situated on the banks of the Chao Phraya River this fabled city is unquestionably one of the most magnificent cities in the world. It was endlessly fascinating.

The growth of Bangkok dates back to 1782 and houses more than five million people. We checked into the elegant Oriental Hotel where the bowing was continuous and the service impeccable. After 6 PM no shorts can be worn in the lobby. Like Venice there are water taxis called long-tails that cruise up and down the river and into back water canals called Klongs. More about the hotel later.

We wasted no time in jumping into a long-tailed motor boat from the Oriental Hotel's private dock with our guide, Tim, who identified the hotels, and public monuments along the river. We felt some teeth shattering river bumps as we sped along on our way to the Temple of Dawn with its towering spires.

At night Tim recommended a buffet dinner at the nearby Sheraton which included a classical Thai performance of music and dance. The serving was lavish and the food tasty although a bit spicy. The next day Tim took us to the Royal Grand Palaces, once the residence of the Kings of Thailand, a sprawling mass of monuments and spires that were an amazing display of opulence. After Tim made some offerings of jasmine, candles, and lotus blossoms, we walked to the Emerald Buddha, five and a half tons of eighteen carat gold trimmed with emeralds. The Buddha sits on a gilded pedestal cast from a single piece of emerald green jasper. It is Thailand's most sacred religious image. There are over 400 temples in Bangkok representing an infinite variety of marvels. We dined that night in the Oriental Hotel's Lord Jim restaurant. There are eight restaurants in this hotel, a favorite oasis of visiting bankers and businessmen, royalty and heads of state. Built in 1876 it is one of the oldest hotels in the city. Many famous literary figures were past guests such as Joseph Conrad, Somerset Maugham, and Graham Greene. In fact, the original building has been renovated as the Authors' Wing and includes a library containing some of the classic works of these writers. We attended a private cocktail party here which was a fantastic gastronomic preview of things to come.

Day three started with a drive outside the city to the floating market where we climbed into a small boat and cruised the narrow canals. All types of food and crafts are sold from boats on the canal. We sampled some fried bananas and coconut pancakes that were delicious. On the way back we stopped for two-hour dry massages. Then it was the obligatory jewelry store and finally to a men's tailor shop where we had some sport coats whipped up in about fifteen minutes and delivered to the hotel the next day.

That night was a feast at a 3,000 seat restaurant called the Seafood Market. From an almost endless counter that displayed countless varieties of fish, we made our selections and gave it to a waitress. Then we went to our table and a waiter asked how we wanted our selections cooked. Everything is so well organized, the food so wonderful, and the cost so reasonable that it was one of the finest meals we had.

On the last day I opted for some poolside duty while my companions did some last minute shopping. June and I went for a massage at the Oriental Spa located across the river in a separate compound. It was quite different than the first one. The ambiance was classy and the massage girls used oils. They were not shy about moving body parts... and I kind of enjoyed it. That night we were on our own and chose a quiet nearby restaurant in the Shangri La Hotel with Thai food and traditional dancing. We concluded that four days in Bangkok was not enough.

In this miraculous city a tourist could browse for gemstones, silks, lacquer ware, teakwood carvings, and silverware. For the more adventurous tourist, there are tuk-tuks, which are three wheeled taxi vehicles that weave in and out of the traffic affording a view of Thai life at street level. And at the street level I am told there are nine-year old prostitutes. It's a city that has everything. The fascination continued even when checking out of the Oriental. A pint-sized porter carried our bags while quoting Shakespeare in his Thai accent. It blew me away.

The Far East II – Bangkok To Yokohama

Elephants that dance in Chiang Mai, Thailand; and monkeys in Malaysia that retrieve coconuts from tall trees were among the astonishing sights June and I witnessed on our return trip to the Far East.

We sandwiched the 16-day REGAL PRINCESS cruise with four days in Thailand and the final days in Japan. With an overnight in Los Angeles and a couple of long flights, we were gone for 28 days.

Back To Bangkok - and off to Elephant Land

Returning to The Oriental Hotel after a hiatus of almost three years, we received a warm welcome and were invited to their private cocktail party in the unforgettable Authors Lounge. We recalled the library whose shelves were stocked with the likes of Conrad, Maugham, and Kipling. One could almost feel the rarified literary atmosphere.

Once we settled in it took no time for June to seek out some choice trinkets at the open market near the Indra Regent Hotel. I chipped in with a couple of sport coats whipped up in a couple of hours. Since the temperature in Bangkok ranged from 96 to 98, I couldn't wait to get into a swimsuit. However in my haste I neglected to take the camera out of my bathing trunks so it was goodbye, Minolta. Our shopping trek that afternoon included a new Nikon. The next day was a side trip to Chiang Mai.

Chiang Mai is in Northern Thailand, more suburban and less frantic than Bangkok. We got there on a Thai jet in one hour. We were ushered around the city by our guide, Chip, a young Thai fellow who giggled at everything I said. A Woody Allen I am not but in Chip's company I was ready to polish my standup routine and take it on the road. Every innocent quip was met with a hilarious outburst. Yet his face waxed disbelief when I tried to convince him that there are no jungles in the USA.

Chip led us to the Maesa Elephant Camp where a bevy of these thumping goliaths were performing in a large field before a clapping, appreciative audience. The elephants did some miraculous things like dancing in a conga line, kicking soccer balls, and bowing to acknowledge the applause. They even made music out of harmonicas placed in their trunks.

After these preliminaries, we thought we were ready. Riding camels in Cairo, donkeys in Santorini, and braving the rapids in Alaska, riding on the back of these gentle slow moving animals seemed like a piece of cake. For June and I it became a 60 minute white knuckle affair astride an 80 year old beast who moved nonchalantly up a steep rocky incline

Stan and June in Chang Mai, Thailand

and then downhill on a road of slippery stones in what seemed like a slow torturous roller coaster with seats that wobbled in all directions. Finally the ride seemed to level off and stopped. It stopped in a little brook, where I thought we would be indelicately plopped into a watery finale. And me with my new camera in my pocket. But our driver managed to get us to the dry exit platform. On our feet again there was Chip laughing in convulsions as he watched our pained expressions throughout the whole ordeal.

Back in Bangkok we found the city not conducive to walking. The sidewalks are narrow though augmented by red bougainvilleas, orchids, and palms. Traffic is abominable and buildings are not architectural wonders. You could find greasy auto repair shops flanked by nice restaurants and fine clothing stores. We passed on the fantastic Buddhas and the Grand Palace having seen them on our previous trip.

Bangkok for us was essentially zesty food, dining on a terrace overlooking the River of Kings, the floating market, a couple of memorable massages, and our transportation on three-wheeled tuk-tuks winding their way through the alleys and choked streets. And all this framed by the memories of the elegant Oriental Hotel.

What's A Trip Without A Cruise?

Our journey by sea began on THE REGAL PRINCESS, a stately eleven year old ship recently refurbished but lacking some of the innovations of the newer ships, like an internet café.

The biggest lack for June was the lack of casino players. Yet there was enough action in the trivia games and energy in the production shows to satisfy the old, the young, and whoever. Thus we left Bangkok to begin our seven country swing through the Orient. We welcomed the sea days on the itinerary.

After a day at sea Kuantan was our first port of call, on the east coast of Malaysia and major port for the export of rice, timber and rubber. For us it was a peaceful village with unspoiled beaches, demonstrations of kite flying, top spinning contests, and the sport of Kung Fu. At the Swiss Garden Resort Hotel we viewed a mock wedding ceremony complete with authentic music and bridal garments.

Fascinating Singapore

At the tip of the Malay peninsula lie the 55 islands of Singapore. Japan occupied the city from 1942 to 1945 but after the war and rapid economic development, it went from a British Crown Colony to an independent Republic in 1965. Our ship arrived in the early morning docking in the shadows of the downtown skyscrapers. Because of its location, it has become the commercial center of southeast Asia.

It is charming, clean, and diverse in its population, cultures, and languages. British influence is still alive with cricket a popular sport and the

Raffles Hotel a hint of bygone colonial times. But Singapore is thoroughly modern judging from its luxurious hotels and gleaming shops along Orchard Road. June and I chose to do a relaxing cruise along the Singapore river with restaurants and small shops dotting the shoreline. We walked a bit along the immaculate streets, stopped for tea at Raffles before returning to the ship.

On board, we enjoyed a day at sea, as we usually do, recharging our tired bodies and brains preparing for the traditional trivia game challenge. Our impressive trivia group however was no match for another group of six who allegedly had the inside track on "triviamania." But trivia was so popular on the ship that it consistently outdrew Bingo and it was just for the glory or perhaps a PRINCESS mug or key chain. Other fun things on the REGAL were golf putting, bridge, and the spa. Steady workouts at the gym kept my girth down but not enough to keep pace with the dining room games. Meanwhile we cruised the South China Sea heading for Vietnam passing a slew of offshore oilfields.

What A Wonderful World

Louis Armstrong was not thinking of Vietnam when he recorded that song but ironically it is identified with that sorry chapter in history. Phu My is the port for Saigon or Ho Chi Min City and since we had seen Saigon we opted for the tour of the more subdued countryside. After the fishing villages of Vung Tau we headed for Nha Trang, popular for its white beaches and farming areas. Just down the road was where American troops in the thousands disembarked. The bus on the tour was hot and our guide spoke poor English but Vietnam had a peculiar appeal for us. Maybe it was the gentle flow of life, the kids desperately following the bus on their bikes hawking T shirts, postcards "one dolla" and New York Yankees baseball caps, or simply the young well dressed women in their white outfits and cone hats doing their daily chores by bicycle.

Hong Kong, The Ultimate Mall

Whether it's the shopping mania or the frenetic pulse of the six million people, excitement and energy are ever present in this environment. It is the world's ultimate mall hosting hordes of shoppers. Merchandise for sale includes jewelry, watches, clothing, optical goods, cameras, carpets, antiques, and you name it. As the ship glides into the legendary harbor with modern skyscrapers and luxurious hotels hugging the shore the pace and bustle is apparent. The narrow streets beckon with the sound and fury of noodle vendors, fortune tellers, and everything imaginable and unimaginable. On one street corner, a vendor was selling snakes used for plumbing complications.

The city was acquired by Britain in the Treaty of Nanking, 1842 and became important in commerce between China and the West. It was occupied by Japan from 1941 to 1945 but in the aftermath of China's civil war, millions of refugees poured into Hong Kong. Under the Sino-British agreement Hong Kong was returned to China on July 1, 1997, and travelers have not reported any significant difference in its appeal. When shopping gets too tiresome, Cantonese food and any other cuisine on earth can be sampled. Choice tourist attractions are the Stanley Market for shoppers, Victoria Peak for photo shoots, and the Aberdeen Fishing Village for a fun sampan cruise and lunch at the Jumbo Restaurant. While June threaded her way through the Jade Market and the Ladies Market, I visited the domed Space Museum and planetarium. After high tea at the Peninsula Hotel we headed for Ocean Terminal looking for an internet café. Temporarily losing June in the vast terminal, then losing track of the time, we arrived back at the ship breathless, five minutes before departure.

Cosmopolitan Shanghai

We navigated the 63 nautical miles on a tributary of the Yangtze River heading for Shanghai. Meanwhile activities on the ship continued. The three production shows were exquisite dancing affairs. Other shows featured an outstanding female singer; Jenifer Green from Australia with a voice that would make Merman's sound like a whisper.

Shanghai's thirteen million people make it one of the most heavily populated areas of the world.

There is lots of street activity and in a gentle rain we visited the newly completed Shanghai Museum. Exhibits covered every phase of Chinese life and history, arts and crafts. We taxied to the Bund, the main business section of the city and viewed again the architectural examples of European influence. In a nearby park, two Chinese girls tested their English on us and their English was a lot better than our Chinese. Other sights to see in Shanghai included the Children's Palace, the YU Gardens and Old Town, and Nanjing Road, all of which are musts for the first timer.

Pusan, South Korea — Hyundais, Kias, and Eyeglasses

Pusan is the second largest city in South Korea and its leading seaport. High rise buildings Hyundai cars, and Buddhist Temples are everywhere. For veterans of the Korean War Pusan is the solemn site of the U.N. Cemetery, where the graves of 2,000 soldiers from sixteen nations lie in neat rows. Caught in the shopping bustle we settled into an optics shop and came out with four pairs of sunglasses at bargain prices. We were surprised to learn that Koreans used movable type about 200 years before Gutenberg's invention.

Onward To Nagasaki, The Gateway To Japan

We walked along the streets of Nagasaki, rode its buses, talked with its schoolgirls, and mingled with the shopping crowds. It could have been any American city. Nagasaki was and is the gateway to Japan. With its scenic harbor, its glassy bay, and its green covered hills, it was the perfect setting for Puccini's *Madame Butterfly*. Together with seeing the Peace Park Memorial on the spot of the atomic bomb explosion, August 9, 1945, and the atomic bomb museum, we will remember the small moments in Japan: the schoolgirl who gave me her seat on a bus, a woman who helped me carry a suitcase down a flight of stairs, the family that insisted on helping us interpret a railway ticket without knowing any English, and the teenagers on an outing who insisted we take photos with them.

Yokohama, Tokyo, and Kyoto

Leaving the REGAL PRINCESS in Yokohama, the port for Tokyo, we said our goodbyes to our shipmates, took down addresses of people we would probably never see again or at the very least exchanged promises to send photos. We will miss Laine Edwards, the lounge pianist who dutifully and expertly played and sang our nightly requests. We will remember the cock-ney one liners of Jonathan as he long-legged it

Peace Park, Nagasaki

between lounges. We will remember Anita Barton eternally. And thank you, Frank Castiglione, our favorite Cruise Director, for your cheery stories and for assembling such an astonishing cruise staff. It was our second cruise with Frank and Anita and we look forward to a third some day.

Tokyo

Arriving at the sumptuous Imperial Hotel with seven suitcases was not too unusual but for our short stay it seemed a bit ludicrous. I love hotel lobbies. This one was the size of Shea Stadium. We were in the fashionable Ginza section of the city which after dark is transformed into a neon light show of bars, cabarets, and discos. Not far from the hotel is Marunouchi, the business center with headquarters of leading banks and financial firms in rows of glass and steel structures. It is not unlike New York's Park Avenue between 40th and 59th streets.

Soon we were on a bus doing an overview of the town. At the top of a 40 story building we had a view of the city from all directions. Tokyo is arguably the largest city in the world. Next it was the Imperial Palace and the Palace Park with its glorious gardens. We were amazed at the Asakusa shopping mall which is just a long endless street with wall to wall people and vendor tents. We witnessed much cigarette smoking and nicely dressed women as we wended our way through this maze of oriental display. We liked it so much we went back the next day by subway which was an adventure in itself.

That night we toured the Ginza with its broad boulevards brimming with names like Gucci, Prada, Hugo Boss all ablaze in neon as if they were hit shows. We also got an idea of restaurant prices which were astronomical. While our guide books described tempting dishes like Shaba-Shaba, Sukiyaki, and Yakitou, without an English menu we were lost in the world of Japanese symbols. We started ordering food from pictures which proved adventurous but satisfactory. If this was Japan in a recession, I shudder to think of the prices during prosperous times.

Kyoto: Komonos, Kabuki Dolls, and Cell Phones

Next day we boarded the bullet train to Kyoto, a vehicle that zips along at 160 mph. The Kyoto railroad station is a work of immense proportions - exposed steel girders 16 stories high with escalators that link each floor with different retail products. Winding almost to the top the escalator is a veritable stairway to the stars, and soars to the Cube, a restaurant floor where young folks were eating at McDonalds, Subways, and Kentucky Fried Chicken restaurants. We had coffee near a table of four schoolgirls giggling and chatting, each one juggling a cell phone, and making peace signs with their fingers as I snapped their picture. We checked into the New Tokyo Hotel not in the same league as the Imperial but it was O.K. The tour of Kyoto began with the Nijo Castle, built in 1603 and home of the first Tokugawa Shogun. It has been designated a historic relic.

The Imperial Palace was a series of temples and vast stretches of pebbled courtyards. The most moving site was a Shogun's former villa known as

The Gold Pavilion. It is a gold plated structure surrounded by a moat and miniature pine trees planted in tiny islands circling the temple. I took photos from every angle to try to capture the inherent serenity of the place. One of the last stops on our tour was the Kyoto Handicraft Center - seven floors of Japanese art, silks, dolls, fans, kimonos, and souvenirs with an all you can eat restaurant for Western and Japanese appetites.

Nestled amidst the hotels, the narrow streets, and tiny canals of Kyoto are about 1700 Buddhist temples and 300 Shinto shrines. Kyoto was once Japan's capital for more than 1000 years. Shoguns, emperors, and military clans clashed over the years until 1868 when the Emperor was restored and the capital moved to Tokyo. We were a little too late for the cherry blossoms at Philosophers Path and the accompanying geisha dances in the Gion district along the Kamo river. We returned to Tokyo on the bullet and were awed by the Tokyo railroad station, a mammoth five story building bedecked with stores, restaurants, an unbelievable bakery, and a blinding array of souvenir shops. All this and Tokyo Disneyland too. We had one more night in Tokyo and Kabuki theatre would have been nice but it was not being shown. We had a decent meal and said "SAYONARA."

Post Script

If there is one image to take back from the Far East, it is the ubiquitous "cranes." They are everywhere and in every city we visited from Bangkok to Pusan and from Chiang Mai to Shanghai. They symbolized to us not only the feverish pace of construction going on but the ambitious attitudes of the people of the new Asia.

ms Amsterdam

There were some anxious moments leading up to our cruise on the ms AMSTERDAM December 1st. But after she was taken out of service for ten days, scrubbed, and sanitized, we boarded the ship confident that the Norwalk Virus was eradicated.

Precautions were still in order and introductions to the Captain specified no handshakes, only elbows. And up on the Lido Deck's buffet, only crew members were permitted to dish out the food and beverages wearing plastic gloves. So it was cruising as usual to the Southern Caribbean.

The MS AMSTERDAM is a sister-ship of the MS ROTTERDAM and they share flagship status of the Holland America Line. The centerpiece on the atrium is a giant clock tower representing the positions and movements of various heavenly bodies with maps and models of tracking the Sun, Moon, and Stars as a means of keeping time. It is a combination of beauty and science. Throughout the ship are blazes of color ranging from artistic ovations to traditional seafaring life – reminders of old Amsterdam and the great Dutch painters. After the usual boat drill and customary preliminaries of acclimation, Captain Dirk van den Berg set a southerly course for Half Moon Cay, Holland America's private island in the Bahamas.

We tendered in on a hot sunny day and June and I immediately grabbed some beach chairs under a tree, tasted a bit of that crystal clear Bahamas water and we were off and running at a dizzying pace for the island barbecue.

Early on we gathered our group of twelve in our stateroom for a cocktail party. Now this was a spacious cabin for a couple, large enough for dancing and other shipboard activities with a nice verandah and huge closets and a good sized head. For our cocktail party I wouldn't say it was cramped but at one point I was nibbling on Bernie Lipsky's ear mistaking it for one of the tasty morsels that were generously spread throughout the stateroom. While Bernie was pouring champagne and lecturing on the anatomy of the optic nerve June was giving her best Pearl Mesta hostess bit. The scene had everything but the Marx Brothers.

The ship had all the Holland America features like movies with popcorn at the Wajang Theatre, violins nightly in the dining room, the renowned Royal Dutch Tea, the Java Bar, towels in the restrooms, and bread pudding at the buffet. And then there were the trivia games, a perennial source of fun, win or lose. After a day at sea we anchored in St. Thomas, which is considered the finest natural harbor in the Caribbean or is it the finest natural "shopping" harbor in the Caribbean. Making our way through the teaming seas of jewelry shops, we made it back to the ship just barely solvent. But thanks to June's artistry at the crap table and my modest luck at blackjack, we were back in business.

There was some fine entertainment as always on the Amsterdam paced by Ramona Fisher a Cruise Director of rare poise and beauty. We liked Jonathan's comedy juggling, Jason Chase's singing and humor, and the Indonesian Crew Show. The rather pleasant surprise for us was seeing Justin Miller, a musical rarity on guitar with an innovative program of big band commentary. We remembered his act on other ships playing piano and featuring his singing wife, Smitty. The production shows were lavish and loud with fine dancing, costumes and a fine lead singer, Michelle Doyle. The Broadway show had my vote as the best of the lot.

The other ports were Martinique, Trinidad, and Isla de Margarita which was substituted for La Guaira, a town that had become somewhat unstable. At Margarita, we taxied to a lovely beach hotel with a nice surf. The final port was Curacao with its colorful houses bordering the harbor and where we took the trolley hitting the high spots of Willemstad. There were some impressive fireworks as we left the harbor. That was it for our ten day Southern Caribbean gambit.

The Dirty Dozen in our cabin - The "Amsterdam"

PROFILES

From Brooklyn To Broadway

He toyed at the piano when he was two. At five his parents were told he could never play piano seriously because of fused thumbs, an inoperable birth defect. By 21 in spite of this handicap, Fred Silver was an accomplished performer. He has also composed seven musical shows and published more than 125 songs. He was a voice coach for Bette Midler, John Davidson, Gloria Swanson, Bette Davis, and Elaine Stritch. Now 64, this Boca Raton resident teaches music and theatre at Florida Atlantic University.

During a recent course on American popular music, he captivated more than 150 students in the Lifelong Learning Society's program at FAU. The course was part piano concert and part sing-a-long and this audience needed little encouragement to participate. Mr. Silver usually is in rare voice as he sings and plays some of his personal favorites like "I'll Buy You A Star" written by Arthur Schwartz from *A Tree Grows in Brooklyn*, a Rodgers and Hart tune "Mimi," and

"The Folks Who Live On The Hill," by Jerome Kern and Oscar Hammerstein II.

Mr. Silver was born to middle class Jewish parents in Brooklyn. Tinkering at the piano served to calm this hyperactive child. He played by ear and was self taught in a family with no history of musical talent. When the subject of further musical training arose, the most prestigious piano teacher in Brooklyn told his parents to save their money. They were advised that his fused thumbs would prevent him from playing the piano. But the young man was determined to pursue a career in music, if only to avoid joining the family business. The condition of his hands prevented him from positioning his fingers on the piano in the conventional way. He developed a method by which he could play with his wrists raised above the keyboard and thus was able to play in high school bands and at Boston University.

After he graduated from BU he met Van Cliburn, who was so impressed he advised him to apply at New York's Juilliard School. Of the 5,000 candidates that semester four composers were selected. One of them was Fred Silver. In the early 1960's he became a protege of composer Richard Rodgers who told him, "I wish you a greater career than I ever had.. "Silver's show *For Heavens Sake*, a jazz-blues concoction that starred Thelma Carpenter, won him a national reputation. He wrote choral music, conducted, and supplied piano accompaniment for Broadway auditions. He became so respected that his book *Auditioning For The Musical Theatre* became the bible for the trade. His weekly column for "Back-stage" called "The Auditioning Doctor" established him as the foremost authority on auditions.

He wrote musical revues and was musical director for Julius Monk's Plaza 9 and Upstairs At The Downstairs, posh clubs on New York's East Side, appeared at supper clubs such as Bon Soir, The Blue Angel, The Mermaid Room, and subbed for Bobby Short at the Carlyle Hotel. His FAU course in popular music benefits from his personal acquaintance with major composers and his detailed knowledge of their work. He respects the work of his friend, Steven Sondheim, and *Company* is one of his favorites. He admires Kern, gets a kick out of Cole Porter, and during the current semester he played and sang many Irving Berlin tunes. Listening to the lyrics of Larry Hart was a lesson in poetry.

His auditioning experience produced a story from the Broadway production of "The Rothschilds." To weed out some of the actors who thought they could sing, at Fred's suggestion, the producer asked each candidate to perform Duke Ellington's "Sophisticated Lady" not the easiest song to negotiate. The tune was so difficult that all of the aspirants were weeded out. Consequently they had to be re-auditioned with songs of their own choosing.

His current students have appeared in local productions of "Meet Me In St Louis" and "Carnival." Mr. Silver has attracted considerable appeal in Boca Raton and his classrooms have grown larger and larger. You might say Brooklyn's loss has become Boca's gain.

A version of this article appeared in HAPPY TIMES MONTHLY, 1996

My Yankee Doodle Daddy

I hardly knew my father. It was one of my life's greatest disappointments. I was eleven when he was taken in an ambulance from our Bronx, New York apartment to Beekman Hospital in downtown Manhattan. I never saw him again. He was 52. It was the summer of 1940.

He had developed a heart condition after being involved in a holdup at a cigar store where he was employed. He took a bullet that entered his neck and came out from his arm. I used to watch him as a child when he changed his bandages or merely swabbed the wounds with mercuricrome. He was not able to work after that and I remember him sitting at the corner of our street each day chatting with the policeman on his break or just watching the kids trudging home from school. His life became sedentary and in effect he became a spectator to life. While Dad talked to me about his wounds, he never went into detail about how they got there or that he was shot by a black man. His only explanation to me was that it happened in a holdup. I found out the details from my mother years after he had died. It had a profound effect on me. The fact that he had always called it an accident and no more than that added to my assessment of him as a fair minded person. One of our neighbors called him a "gentleman," which in those day was a rare compliment. To me he was more than that. I thought he was a historian and a teacher.

He would love to recite patriotic poems to me, particularly, "Old Ironsides," by Oliver Wendell

My Dad about 1913

Holmes , about the famous ship, the USS Constitution:

"Aye tear her tattered ensign down,
long has it waved on high ...
And many an eye has danced to see
That banner in the sky."

He knew it by heart and whenever he said those words, I was moved. He did everything but wave the flag. As a small child I would urge him "to say the poem to me," and he would gladly oblige. Or he would do the Preamble to the Constitution. "We the people..."

At the dinner table there were usually political discussions with my older brother. Dad was an old line Roosevelt Democrat and he favored the common man. My brother was a somewhat doubting Democrat and it made for an interesting give and take, as I dimly recall.

Dad was proud that he had a younger brother serving in the peacetime U.S. Navy and when Uncle Abe came by on one of his infrequent visits, Dad was thrilled and I was happy to receive the coins that my uncle would always deposit in my pocket. These are some of the meager memories of my father. His deep-seated patriotism, his love of American history, and his fairness to his fellow man represent a grand legacy my father left me.

Funny Girl, Anita

While women of her age are likely to be puttering in their English gardens, doing charity teas, and attending Covent Garden theatre openings, Anita Barton is having a hell of a time on the REGAL PRINCESS, that never-never land of fun and games, cavorting in her fishnet garb with her cruise staff cohorts at Pub Night. She has also demonstrated "square boxes" in an arts and crafts project, delivered a lecture on "50 ways to wear a scarf without lynching yourself" or presided over a honeymoon get-together for "all couples married one year or less." In the hands of anyone else the yawns would be wider than a mile. Anita sprinkles her talks with that ingenuous British charm and wit usually ending in an off color joke. On our watch - a 16-day jaunt - she sported an extensive evening wardrobe. One night designated as a Chinese theme she was poured into a blazing red long skirt affair with the traditional high Chinese collar. It was a knockout. Cameras were clicking at her all night.

Anita's duties extend to chairing the Captain's Circle Hospitality Desk and distributing prizes at the Captain's cocktail party for passengers with the most PRINCESS cruises under their belt. So she is a lot more than a social hostess since the job is no longer a person who dresses up and sits at the Captain's dinner table and introduces passengers to the Captain trying to make them feel like "we're all buddies, aren't we?" She is a member of the Cruise Staff and is a body and soul entertainer.

It probably stems from her early aspirations to be on the stage. However, "Mum" didn't think that was a proper occupation for a young English lady. Instead, Anita split from her comfy London digs and signed on with the QE2 as a casino lady and all around deck hand. Having just about circled the world, she still gets excited about travel. Among her greatest thrills was seeing the Great Wall of China and the Pyramids in Egypt. She has vivid memories of hugging a baby orangutan in Singapore and unintentionally arousing a lovable dolphin in Sydney. How many possible mates she has aroused is debatable but she confided to me that she had acquired a reputation as a "professional fiancee."

She is petite, friendly and affectionate and it shows by her apt smile and the perennial "dahling." It's not always the Gracie Fields English Music Hall demeanor, the job has its serious side. She feels one of her main functions is "to communicate with the singles and get them involved so that they can share in the fun for a better cruise experience." When I asked facetiously "what do you want to be when you grow up" she replied without a pause, "I haven't yet decided. There's plenty of time for that." She might just be the Peter Pan of the cruise industry.

One of her best routines was the Regal's rendition of *The Weakest Link*. Anita was as stone faced as Anne Robinson but by far much funnier. She hosted a "Name That Tune" quiz. Her patented hints were provocative and win or lose the passengers in the audience had a great time. And what do you think she does when she goes home to England on holiday? Anita Barton putters around in her English garden.

Kiss Me Katie

Getting a dancer down on paper is almost impossible. In the case of Kate Ferguson, who I met while she was doing library duty on the MILLENNIUM, the transformation was delicious.

She had the usual pedigree of a dedicated dancer: the pushy English parents, training at London's Studio Centre, experience in modeling, television, and West End chorus lines. Then it was dancing in *For Me and My Gal*, *42nd Street*, and even singing four lines in *Les Mis*. Finally she signed on with the cast of CELEBRITY'S GALAXY. From there it was an easy trip to the new MILLENNIUM.

As she told it, "a dancer's life has its moments... some exasperating, some amusing, and some embarrassing." Kate explained that in one show, the chorus had to wear top hats and hers didn't fit too snugly. When it inevitably toppled off, she had to scamper around the stage to retrieve the irretrievable bowler. It added a comic touch to a serious ballet. The audience howled but later Kate had to face the demonic gaze of the dance captain.

Another example of the hard life of a hoofer was when Kate put on a costume, flitted on stage, and realized she was still wearing the coat hanger inside the costume. "Damn uncomfortable."

The most embarrassing moment occurred after an unbelievably fast costume change. "I forgot to put on my undergarments," Kate explained, "and had to do some high kicking, can-can routine. It was a bit drafty, to say the least," and Kate did not have to wonder why there was thunderous applause from the first three rows.

Hip Hop, Tap Tap

Samantha Lupien has been dancing from the age of two. Since her parents own The Canadian Dance Studio in Toronto, not only was dancing in the genes but in the family business. Before signing on with the MERCURY which was her first cruise ship, she taught, choreographed, competed, and danced in major industrials all across the U.S. So at the ripe old age of twenty she sees herself as an accomplished dancer.

Nailing her on the last day of our cruise at the Tastings Bar, she was glib, attractive and at times wore an ingratiating grin like a kid getting her first doll. She seemed a bit relieved that her contract on the ship was nearing a close and when I asked her: "what's the next stop for your dancing feet?" She said "the first thing is to go home and become reacquainted with my family. Then I'll take all my videos and demos and pursue some connections in New York."

While she has run the gamut of every dance style from jazz to hip-hop, she actually loved the challenges on the MERCURY stage. As the lead dancer she had the responsibility of blocking (positioning) the dancers for each number. And in the event that a dancer leaves and is not replaced immediately, it is her job to re-block the dances and that means more rehearsals and less time off. But she does not complain. On a seven day cruise, there are four shows and the dancers have three days off. Nobody else on the staff gets the privilege of a full day off. She sensed some resentment at this since the dancers are usually the youngest and earn the highest salaries.

One of the perks of the lead dancer is she gets her own cabin while the other dancers must share a room. Samantha takes her job seriously and studies videos of every show. We discussed the dress code and the behavior code that the dancers must adhere to. "Suspicions of too much partying could lead to a breathalator test which could mean immediate dismissal. It did happen to one of our dancers."

She seemed to agree with me about the uneven calibre of the four shows all produced by Opryland out of Nashville. The 'Bond Voyage' I felt was overloaded with sound, smoke, and a lot of technical activity tied together loosely by a few undistinguished tunes from James Bond movies. A better show was "On Broadway," which seems to get raves on every ship we've been on. One of the particular joys for Samantha on the cruise was giving dancing lessons to the children ages ten to eighteen. "They go for hip-hop and it's a lot of fun," she said. Another sideline of her role as dancer was taking the kids on a back-stage tour.

But onstage, back stage, or off stage I found her to be a charming person and a gracious interviewee.

Make Up Your Mind, Lori

Remember the dream sequence in OKLA-HOMA? That's where the title comes from in this verbal snapshot of Lori Seymour, the Cruise Staff Recreational Coordinator who presided over the daily trivia bouts on the MS ZUIDERDAM. The key word is "bouts" since some of the players will display anger or shed a tear if not on the winning end of a HOLLAND AMERICA key chain or luggage tag. But Lori is a calm, confident administrator who knows when to compromise if a trivia response from a player may barely miss its mark.

Picture the looks of a young Mary Martin with prominent cheek bones and a ready smile, somewhat like a Canadian sunset. She hails from a town called Sussex in New Brunswick, Canada, holds two degrees from St. Thomas University in St. John (a BA in English and a BED in Education) and is part of a large family of brothers, sisters, nieces, nephews, cats and what have you. Growing up in a small town with a population of just a bit more than the capacity of the MS ZUIDERDAM she boasted of her volley ball expertise and reading Jane Austen novels. This is her first contract on a cruise ship and her first contact with the world outside of New Brunswick. She finds the long hours as a member of the cruise staff exhausting and has not decided on her next assignment. (Hence, the title.)

Her next step could be on the staff of the PRINSENDAM's world cruise, or a teaching position in England, or going back to her social work job in New Brunswick. However, after meeting Lars, a Dutch engineer on the ship, the next offer could very well be marriage and a home in Holland. Whatever she decides we wish her well. Perhaps she'll need a dream sequence before she "makes up her mind." We'll always remember her laughter in the Windstar Lounge managing the tempers and terrors of a roomful of seniors engaged in the trivia battle. Lori had a special request that I never received from others I have interviewed. It was a wish that I do a follow up to this interview sometime after she has made her career decision. "Don't take too long, Lori; I'm not getting any younger."

The Trivia Diva

1. What member of the STATENDAM's cruise staff is ebullient, bright and looked ravishing in a red low cut evening gown at the Captain's dinner?

2. What member of the STATENDAM's cruise staff awards the most fabulous prizes?

3. What member of the STATENDAM's cruise staff wears a tiara to designate her majestic status?

The answer to each of the above trivia questions is COURTNEY RELIHAN, the trivia diva, the blonde vivacious talkative jumping bean who administers the 20 brainteasers each morning at the Crow's Nest lounge. This indefatigable Iowan born, Chicago bred, Northwestern University Theatre Arts major never stopped pacing. She sings, dances, plans, and is unsinkable whether she's doing trivia or quoit throwing, shuffleboard or as the ship D.J. And all of these activities come to her as naturally as breathing. Courtney was an activist in high school and college organizing clubs or trips and performing in shows like *The Boy Friend* and *Oklahoma*. She loves travel and spent some time in London and Los Angeles before she decided to inhabit the happy world of cruising.

With three brothers in the family, she had to keep moving, to stay competitive athletically as well as academically. For a 24 year old she is quite mature and poised, that is, once I glued her to an Ocean Bar chair for this interview. While she enjoys contemporary music, she adores the Broadway show tunes. What surprised me was her selection of Judy Garland as her favorite performer. Her life plan has not yet materialized but after graduate school at Yale or NYU, she would like to pursue a career in event planning or some type of non-profit work. But Courtney is keeping her options open. Marriage, of course, is still on the horizon and a definite part of her life plan. But the guy who gets her had better be up on his trivia game.

A True Football Hero

Jewish football players are a rare commodity. Today's fans root for Jay Fiedler, the Miami Dolphin's successor to Dan Marino. Some years back Allie Sherman was the Jewish entry on the New York Giants as a left-handed passer and coach. And before that, who can forget Sid Luckman from Columbia University when he established all kinds of "T" formation records with the vaunted Chicago Bears of George Halas?

Rewind to the roaring twenties and the depression thirties and there was the legendary Benny Friedman, born into an orthodox Jewish family in 1905, who pioneered the invention of the forward pass. Thus he was the forerunner of our modern quarterbacks. Benny had played high school football growing up in Cleveland and was recruited by the University of Michigan. When he graduated in 1926, the 5'10" - 175 pound Benny Friedman had become the team's first Jewish captain and a two time All American selection. He led his team through three near perfect seasons and revitalized the game by his proficiency in throwing what was in those days a kind of blob-like ball.

The game in those years was a static, grind-it-out affair with repetitive running plays livened up by an occasional lateral or a surprising drop kick. He had decided while in his freshman year at Michigan that what the varsity team needed was a good forward passer.

Consequently he sharpened his passing skills and developed an uncanny accuracy in picking out receivers. His successful passing in his collegiate and professional years opened up the game and popularized it to what it has become today, one of the most exciting spectator sports of our time. It has also led to the construction of a score of stadiums some holding as much as 100,000 fans.

And yet Benny Friedman was more than just a passer. When he signed on to play professional ball with the Cleveland Bulldogs playing a 21-game season going 60 minutes each game, he was a star attraction. He completed passes from all over the field, ran with reckless abandon and excited the crowds. Tim Mara, the New York Giants owner, who was awash in money-losing seasons, saw his value and lured him into signing with the Giants in 1928 at $10,000 per year. This gave the New York Giants a Jewish quarterback in a Jewish city and was a key factor in Mara's fortunes eventually being reversed. In his six years as a pro Benny passed for 5,653 yards and 55 touchdowns with the runnerups not even close.

In 1933, Mayor LaGuardia convinced him to coach football at City College at $4,500 a year. There were several winning seasons with players who had never played football, who didn't know the terminology, and who nevertheless packed in the fans at Lewisohn Stadium. Friedman entered the Navy in 1942 and after the war joined the faculty at Brandeis University as athletic director and football coach. He remained there until 1963. Red Grange called him "The best passer who ever lived." Paul Gallico referred to him as "the Babe Ruth of football." In spite of his feats, Benny Friedman lost his battle with the NFL to include pre-1958 players in its pension plan.

Suffering from diabetes and having a leg amputated, a depressed Benny Friedman committed suicide in 1982. In a note he left behind, this battling, forgotten man wrote that he didn't want to end up as "the old man on the bench."

Source: "Battlin' Benny" by Willard Manus, The CCNY Alumnus, Winter 2002.

The Houseguest

He was a man possessed of magic. He could perform miracles. To my wife, there was nothing he couldn't repair or construct. I could even say, Pat saved my marriage.

Who could not love a man who was able to fix my garden hose so that my wife did not look like a wet T- shirt ad when she washed the patio, or at the drop of a high hat could change the high ceilinged light bulb in ten seconds without doing a swan dive from a fifteen foot ladder, or repair a sink faucet after a leak became something resembling Victoria Falls, or resurrected my TV and VCR after a disastrous power failure had reduced our after dinner activity to reading and radio recreation?

Such a man is Pat. Not a neighbor, not a relative, but a super friend who had come south to witness some baseball spring training games but became the third member of my family for a few days. Unlike the anthem that after three days, a houseguest begins to stink like a fish, my wife wouldn't let him go until she listed for him a few things I was incapable of doing or ill equipped as a city boy to do. Who knows how long I could have survived without him?

For example, he tightened the screws on the toilet seats permanently after I had slipped and splattered myself all over the bathroom floor. One night we were all sitting out on the patio as darkness was descending and my wife said "I can hardly see the garden when it gets dark." Like a knee jerk reaction, Pat's brain sprung into action and the next night our little patch of grass and palm trees became the Hanging Gardens of Babylon. She almost cried when Pat inserted the plug and the backyard was suddenly lit as quickly as the tree in Rockefeller Center.

One particularly windy day he was taking a leisurely stroll, smoking his pipe when the mail was being delivered. As the mail truck left, letters and magazines started blowing all over the street because the weather-beaten mail box was cracked and disintegrating. Like a flash Pat reconstructed the shabby box hammered it together, repainted it and now, voila, we can boast of having a mail box that's the envy of South Florida. It wouldn't have looked better if I had purchased a new one.

I don't want to give the impression that Pat is a one dimensional man. He is a respected and retired academic. But his creativity flows from his brain to his hands. To me he is as artistic as Picasso, as creative as Andy Warhol painting soup cans. To illustrate, one morning I had spied him groping around in the garbage. We had filled the refrigerator with lots of food and snacks so I wondered what he was looking for. I later learned that he had snared a discarded plastic ketchup bottle to concoct insulation for the electric outlet that he had buried in the grass when he installed the flood-lights in the garden. Within the same garbage heap, he managed to salvage a broken flag pole. He shaped this into a reinforcement for a somewhat creaky antique chair.

These feats may not seem Bunyanesque to the run of the mill homeowner. I viewed them differently because of the special relationship I had with Pat. I considered them collectively as mans' humanity toward man. Pat used to tell me "a man is as good as his tools." The tools that I supplied him with were a pair of pliers, a screwdriver, and a toy hammer. That's all Pat needed.

Before he went back home, we enjoyed a beer together. I toasted this giant of a man who was more like a genie than a giant. All I could say was "Thanks, Buddy, " My wife had a few more comments to make and anticipating more unexpected breakdowns said, "Come back real soon, ya hear."

Ravishing Ramona

If Doris Day was a Cruise Director, she'd be Ramona Fisher. Cool, calm, and truly enchanting she could have come out singing 'Sentimental Journey' and given a convincing impersonation. But Ramona played it straight as Cruise Director on the MS AMSTERDAM with a couple of smooth lines, a fabulous smile, and a promise to bring out some fine entertainers over the next ten days.

I caught up with her in her office while planning assignments on her laptop and looking delightfully businesslike. We hopped over to a nearby bar where she expounded willingly on the life and times of Ramona Fisher. I must confess that when she was first introduced in the Show Lounge as the band played "Ramona," one of my old, old favorite tunes, I thought, shades of a strip show. But there she was decked out in her blonde Dutch Boy hairdo eloquently dishing out the pleasures of cruising on the MS AMSTERDAM.

Ramona hails from Pennsylvania, attended Penn State College and after getting out with a major in theatre arts, she said: "what'll I do now?" So she tried her luck in some regional Samuel

Beckett plays, serious avante garde stuff but not exactly burning up the boards. She followed that up with a stirring appearance in Edward Albee's *The Sand Box* where she was all but hidden in a pile of sand. She managed to show off some more interesting body parts when she got to Los Angeles as an extra in a flick called *Quick Change*. You might have missed that one at your local Muvico or Blockbuster. Along the way she did a stretch of teaching which she thought rewarding and tried a couple of marriages that didn't work out.

Ramona really hit her stride in Tampa when she became part of a singing group called the "R" Girls. The "R" did not refer to the rating of their performance. The group consisted of three singers with names beginning with "R." Clever touch, yes? The group did radio commercials and local television shows and then migrated north to Manhattan's Piano Bars. So the logical question is: How come a cruise ship? Her first seagoing stint was actually as a big band singer on the QE2 with the Mark Joyce orchestra. From there it was on the staff of the REGAL PRINCESS... and how in the world did I not notice her when I was on the very same ship? A newcomer on the AMSTERDAM, she has won her sea legs and whether she sings, emotes, or just looks pretty while introducing the entertainment, this versatile "R" girl is resourceful, responsible, and ravishing to behold – a person destined for success on the high seas.

Eric Stone - Peerless Pianoman

Once upon a time there was a pianoman. He was 125 pounds of song and dance with an uncanny talent for holding an audience spellbound. He did it by singing and playing out just about all the parts in *La Cage* or *Les Mis* and a slew of other Broadway hits recalling memories that had been safely tucked away in the windmills of our minds.

With his big voice, his piano, and his theatrics booming out from his Deck 7 perch on the SUN PRINCESS, we couldn't help but be impressed. And every night thereafter, Jeanie's little 38-year old Eric had us entranced with a Pinza-like basso, a Channing vibrato, or a Streisand medley, catching the humor and the pathos of the shows.

Was it the gentle dip of the head, the timely giggle, the gracious "thank you's," his love of entertaining that captured our fancies? I sat with 20 or 30 other mesmerized faces listening to his theatrical valentines gleaned from a trunkful of tunes - no, not tunes - performances. All this that began with a used piano his father trucked in one night in Cleveland. All this from the inspiration and encouragement of his Grandma Zelda.

Not from the Cleveland Institute of Music or the Kent State music scholarship did the knack of stirring an audience emerge. Perhaps the nurturing came from his experience in dinner theatres, or the Sondheim benefit, or his eleven month stint in *A Chorus line*, or his days with Gower Champion and Nureyev. He learned it mainly by growing up in Cleveland, not on a ball field with the other kids, but on his second hand piano. The chord games were his ball games. He played hard and fast and woke up sometimes in the middle of the night to practice, to play, to get it right and if he didn't - it was great fun.

Eric got it right, loving every moment on the SUN PRINCESS from 9 PM until his fingers or voice weakened. He knew nothing of breaks or union rules. He would play for nothing. When I requested an Arlen tune, it evoked a Garland "Over The Rainbow" mood and Kern's "All The Things You Are" was equally as evocative. He didn't have to tell me of his gratitude to Judy, or his emulation of Peter Allen or Sammy. I could see him as a fantastic *Pal Joey* on stage. His love of music, dancing, and theatre was infectious and every performance showed all the weapons of his musical arsenal. He betrayed one wish, however: a wish if only Grandma Zelda could see him now.

Michele Doyle

It was easy to spot Michele on the stage of the M.S. AMSTERDAM's theatre. She sounded like Streisand but looked a lot prettier and younger. And when she warbled Harold Arlen's bluesy "Come Rain or Come Shine," I knew I had to interview her. So oddly enough I met this lovely, tall, shapely, green-eyed gal in the ship's Library while she was doing her extra chores. Our meeting went like this:

STAN: So you seem to be a singing librarian like Barbara Cook in "The Music Man."

MICHELLE: Not quite. Part of my job on the entertainment staff is to check out the books on certain days. Over the last ten days, however, when the ship was taken out of service because of the Norwalk Virus, the entire cast helped the crew in scrubbing every corner of the ship from the elevator buttons down to the last book in the library.

STAN: You actually swabbed the bookshelves? How did that ten-day break affect the cast and the production shows?

MICHELE: Three people in the cast got the virus and were quarantined; there were some replacements brought in and adjustments to some of the dance numbers had to be made.

STAN: The shows I've seen seemed to go over seamlessly. Have you ever experienced any embarrassing moments like forgetting a lyric or forgetting a vital part of a costume?

MICHELE: (Breaking into an appealing girlish grin) Thank God, no.

STAN: How do you handle the romantic duets?

MICHELE: The boys in the cast, the singers and dancers, are great and supportive. I find my acting ability helps in many situations.

STAN: Tell me about your singing career. Where and how did it start?

MICHELE: When I was in first grade in St. Johns, Newfoundland at the age of seven, I sang "I'm Getting Nothing For Christmas" in a school concert. Since then I have acquired a Bachelor's degree in Music from Memorial University of Newfoundland. I have been performing for many years in St. Johns and Toronto. My most recent show was *The Beggar's Opera* with the Soul Pepper Theatre Co.

STAN: Was music in the genes?

MICHELE: My Mom and Dad are musicians, my brother is a professional musician, and my other brother plays guitar and sings just for fun. I also have a sister and I am the youngest.

STAN: So growing up, the sounds of music were everywhere. Do you have a favorite singer?

MICHELE: I have many. I admire Judy Garland and enjoyed singing "Over The Rainbow" on the AMSTERDAM's World Voyage in a show called "Personality, Too."

Late Rally

STAN: Another Arlen tune and another Judy Garland fan. I have found overwhelming admiration for Judy Garland from the singers I have interviewed. What's over that rainbow in your career?

MICHELE: My contract expires next month and I'll go home to the family. Then I will continue to sing and act and try to grow as an artist.

MUSIC

All The Things You Are

Words by
OSCAR HAMMERSTEIN IInd

Music by
JEROME KERN

"All The Things You Are"

All The Things You Are

I have been infatuated with a song, not just any song. I consider it "a classic." It was written in 1939 for a Broadway show called *Very Warm For May*. The show is lost in oblivion but the song survived. The music was written by Jerome Kern, one of America's earliest composers of popular songs and whose reputation for melody is legendary. The lyrics were conceived by Oscar Hammerstein II, before his partnership with Richard Rodgers, and are sheer poetry. The song: "All The Things You Are," an homage to a loved one without the word "love" even mentioned. "You are the promised kiss of springtime, "he wrote," that makes the lonely winter seem long." And then, "You are that breathless hush of evening that trembles on the brink of a lovely song." It has the imagery of a Shakespeare sonnet.

In the life span of the average popular tune, the shelf life is a mere wisp; of the here today, gone tomorrow variety. But some songs acquire an elongated life and are lifted to a category called "standards." Examples are Hoagy Carmichael's "Star Dust" and Harold Arlen's "Over The Rainbow." In this lofty category, on most music expert's "ten best list" lies my favorite, "All The Things You Are." The tune still lives on played by dozens of cocktail lounge pianists, and wherever and whenever relief from modern music is desired. I've heard it in the piano bars of cruise ships and from a selection of elevator music in a dentist's office.

But it wasn't until some time in the 1970s that the tune affixed itself to my mind. It was at this time that I acquired the sheet music for the tune at a tag sale from the attic of a house in Hewlett, Long Island. The owners were relocating and emptying their attic of an assortment of "trash." The old adage used by sponsors of such tag sales is "one man's trash is another man's treasure." This was my treasure purchased together with a stack of old 78 RPM records and dusty picture frames. It wasn't until I sold my house in Lido Beach, Long Island and emptying my own trash that I rediscovered the frayed-edged sheet music of "All The Things You Are." I began to sing it, I played it on the piano, I requested it whenever I was at a cocktail lounge or weddings or affairs, and it became a veritable obsession. The tune represented Jerome Kern at his melodic best, Hammerstein at the top of his word game. It was not a simple melody not easy to sing having a wide range and key changes in the release. I think only great singers like Maureen McGovern and Rosemary Clooney recorded it with any great success. And Maureen's hitting and holding that final note gave me the shivers. My late wife grew to love it and played it on the piano mixing it in with Chopin and Schubert. When she died, I took one of Hammerstein's phrases in the lyric and engraved it on her footstone. It read: "the dearest things I know are what you are." It was the most gracious tribute I could think of for a wife of 36 years.

I rarely hear it these days and it has taken on for me a sacred meaning, almost like a prayer. I have stopped requesting it because it makes me sad and I don't feel I should burden anyone else with my sadness. But the tune will live forever with me, as one of the dearest things I know.

Bing Crosby, The Legend

From the frantic prohibition years to the dark depression days of the 30's, America's most beloved entertainer was Bing Crosby. He was your average regular guy and a symbol of everyone's ambition.

He was veritably a pioneer who could sing in any style from minstrel and spiritual songs to tin pan alley, blues and country, even patriotic and Irish lullabies.

There was a time... when it was said that no hour of the day or night, year after year, passed without the voice of Bing Crosby being heard somewhere on this earth.

From 1935 to 1946 "fifty million" listeners tuned in every thursday night to hear Bing's kraft Music Hall. Compare this to the hottest TV series in 2000, "Who Wants To Be A Millionaire," which peaked at "thirty six million" viewers.

Crosby was the first white vocalist to appreciate and assimilate the genius of Louis Armstrong, his rhythm, his emotion, his comedy. Their first important vocal together was "Heebie Jeebies" in 1926 and "Muddy Water" in 1927.

Bing once told Joe Bushkin (Tommy Dorsey's famous piano player) that "Louis Armstrong was the greatest pop singer in the world, that he was and ever will be."

Crosby compiled 1668 recorded songs. His command over recordings, movies, and radio was unrivaled. Duke Ellington had such an admiration for Bing that he refused to hire a male vocalist until he could find one who sounded a lot like Bing. That was Herb Jeffries.

Bing, like Al Jolson, was unique. Jolson threw himself at his audience. Bing made them come to him.

According to Artie Shaw, "Bing Crosby was the first hip white person in the United States."

On nearly all his recordings, at his radio broadcasts, and in theatres, Bing was backed by guitarist Eddie Lang, who sat at his right elbow, sharing a microphone, steadying him with strummed chords, pacing him with reliable accompaniment.

Bing had insisted that Paramount Pictures include Eddie Lang in all his projects. Lang's Paramount contract, as a result, netted him $15,000 per Crosby picture plus a salary of $1,000 per week while touring. He was the highest paid sideman in the industry.

The original orchestra on the Kraft Music Hall before John Scott Trotter was Jimmy Dorsey's. The drummer in the Dorsey Band was named Spike Jones who later fronted a group called the City Slickers.

Bing had a love of southern things. He married two southern belles and his long time buddy was Phil Harris whose theme song was "That's What I Like About The South."

While touring with the Paul Whiteman Band, in Philadelphia, he met two chorus girls named Ginger Meehan and Dolores Reade. He had a brief fling with Ginger who later became Mrs. Johnny Mercer. Dolores Reade became Mrs. Bob Hope.

Bing mentioned as the most important musical influences in his life – Jolson, Armstrong, and Bix Beiderbecke (the legendary cornetist.)

Bing made a record of "Ol' Man River" shortly after show boat opened at the Ziegfeld Theatre on Dec. 27, 1927. He sang it an octave higher than Paul Robeson did and Bing recalled it as one of his best recordings.

Bing recorded with all of these artists at one time or another: Paul Whiteman, Sam Lanin, Dorsey Brothers, Matty Malneck, John Scott Trotter, Duke Ellington, Gus Arnheim, Victor Young, Don Redman, Isham Jones, Lennie Hayton, etc.

He also recorded with: Guy Lombardo, Jimmy Grier, Nat Finston, Georgie Stall, Jimmy Dorsey, Dick McIntyre, Harry Owens, Bob Crosby, The Andrew Sisters and Vic Schoen, Joe Venuti, and lest we forget from the movie *High Society*, Grace Kelly ("True Love") and Frank Sinatra ("Have You Heard.")

Source: Gary Giddons – Crosby, **The Early Years, Pocket Full of Dreams.**

My Twelve Best... And His

My ten best American popular tunes would probably never get the unanimous support of any musicologist, but, I would defend them to the death. These were not easy selections and as Will Friedwald states in his 2002 *Stardust Melodies*, "it would have been easier to do a book of Irving Berlin songs than to pick out just a few." But, I have not been so timid and my selections come from the heart and an ear that has been attuned to them from my saxophone playing days a hundred years ago. Mr. Friedwald's choices are understandable, in a sense, since his aim was to write "a biography of twelve of America's most popular songs."

I have added two more to my ten best so it will be interesting to compare my choices with his. We agree on "Star Dust," "St. Louis Blues," and "Stormy Weather." His choice of "Mack The Knife" is certainly odd, the tune having been written in Germany before Kurt Weill ever saw Shubert Alley or even Tin Pan Alley. But with a history of Louis Armstrong's recordings as well as Bobby Darin's, and a successful show, it's latent popularity was assured. But, not in my book.

Another entry I would dispute is Herman Hupfield's "As Time Goes By." While I love the song and the mood it evokes, it's popularity stems only from the movie, *Casablanca*, which revived a dead song written in 1931. I found many better songs. I would also take issue with "Night and Day" as a Cole Porter entry. True, it's one of Porter's best and a favorite of singers and musicians and Sinatra called it a "standard classic." However, if you are going for Porter, does anything compare to "Under My Skin?" It was perennially Sinatra's number one request.

"Begin The Beguine" as recorded by Artie Shaw belongs in our heritage and how we all learned the lindy hop. To recall the tune is a rare nostalgic treat. So it gets my vote over "Night And Day" and "Under My Skin" becomes my Number 11.

Richard Rodgers would fill the same category as Berlin and it would be a mortal sin to overlook dozens of wonderful tunes. Surely any of his waltzes would qualify but I picked as my favorite Rodgers tune, "It Never Entered My Mind," with a perfect lyric by Larry Hart and just the right touch of sophistication. I would not quibble with "My Funny Valentine" but there are so many great Rodgers and Hart songs that it hurts to omit any of them. And lest we forget, when Dick brought in Oscar to replace Larry, the material they churned out was not exactly chopped liver. As an example, "It Might As Well Be Spring" would be my number twelve choice.

As Mr. Friedwald points out, "I Got Rhythm" had Merman, a fabulous show, *Girl Crazy*, and a terrific pit band with Goodman, Miller, Krupa, and Jimmy Dorsey. It's been played and sung by everyone, but, the Gershwins deserve a better entry musically. "Someone To Watch Over Me" is just a superior song introduced by Gertrude Lawrence and sung today by any night club singer worth her salt. Moreover, "The Man I Love," would have been a better choice for Will since it had a storied past before it flowered as a Gershwin favorite. "Summertime" belongs in the opera category and even as a popular song doesn't rank with the best of Gershwin.

Strayhorn's "Lush Life" simply doesn't belong in this rarified company of songs. "Body and Soul" was a decent choice and has been done, redone, and overdone by so many musicians and singers that the song is as old hat as the Hawkins record that I wore out many years ago. What is unforgivable is the omission of "All The Things You Are" from anyone's popular list. It is Jerome Kern at his mature 1939 best, the only survivor from the flop show, *Very Warm For May*. The melody is simple with a tricky release and Hammerstein's ode is a step away from Keats' "Grecian Urn." As an Irving Berlin entry, "Alexander's Ragtime Band" would have given Will Friedwald an awful lot to write about as one of Berlin's earliest hits and most endurable songs. I have no argument with "Ol' Man River."

So far from *Stardust Melodies'* selections being a golden dozen, I see some tarnished edges. But any book about songs of this beloved era I warmly welcome. Thanks, Will.

STAN'S	WILL'S
Star Dust	Star Dust
St. Louis Blues	St. Louis Blues
It Might As Well Be Spring	My Funny Valentine
Stormy Weather	Stormy Weather
All The Things You Are	Summertime
It Never Entered My Mind	Body and Soul
Alexander's Ragtime Band	I Got Rhythm
Begin The Beguine	Night And Day
I've Got You Under My Skin	Lush Life
Someone To Watch Over Me	Mack The Knife
Sophisticated Lady	As Time Goes By
Blues In The Night	Ol' Man River

Big Band Notes

GLENN MILLER – How I wish I could have been at the Glen Island Casino, New Rochelle, New York in May of 1939 when the Glenn Miller Band reached its zenith of popularity. I was a bit too young but I had heard about it from my older brothers. It did not come easy for the Miller band. Glenn had paid his dues working as an arranger, a trombonist, and making several attempts as a band leader before the breakthrough at Glen Island. Working with Tommy Dorsey and Benny Goodman in the 1930s Ben Pollack band as well as the Ray Noble band he found himself later in the pit band of *Girl Crazy*, the 1930 Gershwin hit show. He learned his jazz from Armstrong, Henderson, and a variety of black musicians.

Miller had studied music with Joseph Schillinger, who also taught George Gershwin as well as Vladimir Dukelsky (Vernon Duke) who composed "I Can't Get Started" and "April in Paris." With his early bands he was seeking a sound that was original and he found it in 1938 by introducing a lead clarinet in his reed section. He added Tex Beneke, Wilbur Schwartz, and Al Klink to his sax section and the Miller band came up with an original syrupy sound that caught on. When Victor Records recognized its commercial value, it rolled out hit records like "Moonlight Serenade," "Serenade in Blue," and "Sunrise Serenade" which fed the desires of the slow dance romantics. The up tempo numbers like "In The Mood" and "Little Brown Jug" featured jazzy trumpet solos and saxophone duels. He brought in arrangers like Jerry Gray, Bill Finegan, and together with Miller himself the band turned out a string of hit records.

The classic "In The Mood" was written by Joe Garland who modeled it after a Wingy Manone riff in 1930 called "Tar Paper Stomp." It worked its way from the Horace and Fletcher Henderson bands before it became "In The Mood." Ironically the tune was first given to Artie Shaw and though he played it, he never recorded it. Miller used Beneke and Klink for the tenor solos and Johnny Best and Billy May for the trumpet solos. It may not have been jazz but America certainly loved it and danced to it. At the peak of his popularity Glenn Miller decided to enlist in the service forming an all star Army Air Force band. He died tragically and mysteriously over the English Channel in December 1944 in an airplane accident that has never been resolved.

TOMMY DORSEY – At New York's Paramount Theatre, the bandstand rose in the wee hours of the morning from its pit, the spot was up on "T. D." playing his familiar theme and just as the bandstand reached its rightful place, there was Ziggy Elman and Chuck Peterson belting out "Well Git It.

That was a typical show and that was "my" New York City as a kid on a Saturday morning spree.

Just like Glenn Miller, Tommy Dorsey struggled for success in the thirties, and went through a similar musical metamorphosis. Although Miller and Dorsey were friends, Tommy was the better trombone player and had a preference for the slow tunes. His theme "I'm Getting Sentimental Over You" is one of the best examples of a sweet almost breathless trombone. After leaving the Dorsey Brothers orchestra, Tommy took over the band of arranger- leader Joe Haymes, and made some fine recordings featuring Bunny Berigan and Bud Freeman. But Dorsey was on the same path as Miller in recording the sweet stuff and a more commercial sound featuring himself in tunes like "Violets For Your Furs," "In The Blue Of Evening," and "There Are Such Things." Swing classics like "Song of India" and "Marie" became hits aided by Bunny Berigan's trumpet solos. When Frank Sinatra joined the band, commercial success was assured.

With the addition of arrangers like Sy Oliver and Paul Weston, singers like Jo Stafford and Connie Haines, drummer Buddy Rich and Ziggy Elman on trumpet, the band achieved the desired balance between jump and sweet numbers. Songs like "I'll Never Smile Again" and "This Love of Mine" sold millions and Sy Oliver arrangements of "Sunny Side of The Street" and "Swanee River" also were big sellers. By the end of 1946, Dorsey along with many other bandleaders was forced to fold. The music business had changed radically. Vocalists were taking over.

ARTIE SHAW – Enigmatic, erudite, and unpredictable, Artie Shaw defied classification. With many unsuccessful attempts at various styles, many critics agree that he was able to form one of the best jump bands in 1939. Helped by Jerry Gray, Buddy Rich, Georgie Auld, and Bernie Privin, Artie's band was at his best and topping Benny Goodman in some of the polls. He envied Goodman's clarinet savvy and sought to reinforce his billing as King of the Clarinet and get out from under Goodman's shadow. Artie formed at least eight different bands between 1936 and 1955 and probably acquired just as many wives. He hired strings in an effort to put a classical touch to the band. He produced "Frenesi" with a band of Hollywood studio musicians. He introduced his Gramacy Five for a jazz flavor with Johnny Guarnieri playing harpsichord. While Goodman played with major symphony orchestras and string quartets, Shaw had to hire his own freelance orchestra for his 1949 Columbia recordings.

In 1938 came his greatest commercial success. It was Jerry Gray's arrangement of "Begin the Beguine," a Cole Porter song from the 1935 show, *Jubilee*. Together with Artie's recording of "Star Dust" with Billy Butterfield's trumpet and a sweet soaring clarinet in 1940, the Artie Shaw band was to be taken seriously. The band played some great music behind Helen Forrest and even Billie Holiday. But Artie Shaw was always searching for a sound he couldn't define and unlike Glenn Miller, he never found it and stopped searching for it.

Strangely and suddenly he walked off the bandstand one night and never returned.

CHARLIE BARNETT – Charlie Barnett was synonomous with "Cherokee" when I was growing up. As a juvenile sax man I used to parrot his staccato style solos while trying to develop my own technique. Like Artie Shaw, Charlie Barnett had a string of marriages - about eleven. But Barnett was financially well healed and pursued a musical life against family wishes. In 1936 he tried a Hollywood movie career but his first love was music. While Miller, Dorsey, and Shaw searched for a particular style, Charlie without shame just emulated Duke Ellington and Count Basie. He didn't consider it plagiarism; he felt it was a tribute to play their tunes, and arrangements. As a saxophonist his model was Coleman Hawkins. In addition his lead trumpet was Robert Burnet who could play the Cootie Williams growl. He actually bought some scores from Ellington and hired Andy Gibson a talented black arranger. In 1939 his most popular record was produced. 'Cherokee,' a tune written by Ray Noble, owed a lot to black musical influences. It became his theme.

Charlie Barnett was the first white band to play the Apollo Theatre in Harlem. While he tried to copy the Ellington sound, in "Rockin' In Rhythm," it fell short of Ellington's joyous style. He was more successful playing in a Basie kick, a straightforward and less subtle style.

In 1944 "Skyliner" became a hit record and like "Cherokee," it used long sustained notes in the melody over a faster background tempo. Charlie's solo at the finish is memorable. In the years when big bands were calling it quits for economic reasons, Barnett kept going, his personal fortune keeping him afloat. In that post war period along with Kenton and Herman, Barnett had one of the most exciting bands with a dynamic rhythm section and some amazing trumpet work by Al Killian. His rendition of "Things Ain't What They Used To Be" is remembered for its effective ensemble work. His last band was an effort at modern Bop but failed to ignite any critical appeal.

GENE KRUPA – Who can ever forget the image of Gene Krupa at the forefront of "Sing Sing Sing" for the Goodman band? However, when Gene Krupa left the Goodman band he relied a bit on vocals and he was fortunate in having Irene O'Day in front of the band. Then in early 1941 Anita O'Day and Roy Eldridge joined the band with more popular appeal. O'Day's voice was considered another instrument and not only a vocal. The influence of Billie Holiday was evident on the slow tunes and she could swing like Ella Fitzgerald as in" Thanks For The Boogie Ride." She teamed with Eldridge on "Let Me Off Uptown." Roy was the traditional Louis Armstrong type and never made the adjustment to the modern Be Bop stuff of Gillespie.

After disbanding in early 1943 Krupa organized another band in a more modern vein, entered the Be Bop era with some fine trumpet work of Red Rodney. I remember Charlie Ventura, a dynamic tenor man from the Hawkins school and the recording of an exciting "Dark Eyes" backed by only Gene on drums and Marty Napoleon on piano. In the 50's Gene worked with smaller combos in a faithful commitment to true jazz. He was a better more disciplined musician, less of a showman, with his own band or combo than when he was with the Benny Goodman band.

Satch

DJ Fred Robbins delivered a eulogy about his friend, Louis Armstrong, saying: "He was truly the only one of his kind, a titanic figure in his own and our time, a veritable Picasso, a Stravinsky, a Casals, a Louis Armstrong."

In his century his influence remade jazz from a folk form into a soloists's art. His influence extended into most aspects of our popular culture - from free jazz to rock and roll to the language and attitudes of fiction.

He set examples for Billie Holiday, Bing Crosby, Frank Sinatra, and Ella Fitzgerald and a dozen others. Miles Davis said: "You can't play anything on the horn that Louis hasn't played." And Dizzy Gillespie said simply: "No him, no me."

And his significance grows steadily. As Louis himself said: "The main thing is to live for that audience cause what you're there for is to please the people."

By the time he joined the Fletcher Henderson band in 1924 he was playing at such an advanced level that the stars in the band like Coleman Hawkins sounded stiff by comparison.

Armstrong changed music. He charted the direction of jazz through the thirties and forties.

Some critics claim that he turned too commercial in his later years and left it to others to refine the art. Yet there would have been no refinement if Louis Armstrong had not created the path.

We Had It All

Just suppose through some astronomical phenomenon you were on the moon in the 21st century and able to peer down at a defined time period on planet earth. In that tiny window from roughly 1935 to 1950 it would have revealed incredible sounds and sights that would immediately signal something special going on that warranted closer study; something that our children and grandchildren in the nineteen eighties and nineties and beyond would never quite understand.

Those special things were sounds wafting across a country at a perilous time in history when America was striving to rescue a world bent on destroying itself... and yet from that nation there were happy sounds from California's Palomar Ballroom to New York City's Paramount Theatre; from Chicago's Pump Room to a parade of college proms; and from the Roseland Ballroom to the Make Believe Ballroom. We the fortunates glued our ears to radios and record players and lindy-hopped or slow-danced, relished Glenn Miller's polished sounds that put us squarely "in the mood." We heard a Benny Goodman trio that made more music from a clarinet, drum, and piano than many sixteen piece aggregations. And we appreciated Ellington's subdued jazz and Basie's unrefined jazz.

This was our music as we went on our way to school, to work, and to play. It was a time of war heroes and peacetime heroes and we needed them. From Harry James and his "Two O'Clock Jump" to Joe DiMaggio's 56 game hitting streak we had our heroes. From Tommy Dorsey to Tommy Henrich, from Woody Herman to Willie Mays in a theatre or in a stadium we came to worship and cheer our heroes. We listened and learned. We memorized Illinois Jacquet's dynamic tenor sax solo on Hampton's "Flying Home" and marveled at Roy Eldridge and his stratospheric trumpet on Krupa's "Let Me Off Uptown." We wore out Coleman Hawkins' unbelievable record of "Body And Soul" from repeated playing.

In the fifties we "doo be doo be dood" with Sinatra and scatted along with Torme. We sat through a rash of mediocre movies at the Paramount Theatre to get another glimpse of the gorgeous Peggy Lee and one more chorus of "Why Don't You Do Right." This music was the oil in our engines and we took it for granted, like Heinz Ketchup and Wonder Bread, that it would never go away. We subscribed to Downbeat Magazine to get the real stories just as we devoured Arthur Daley's sports column in the New York Times or Jimmy Breslin's observations in the New York Post.

We were slaves of the city's symphonies with its cars' tooting horns and radios blasting from apartments and kids playing stoop ball or stick ball or girls jumping double dutch. We were not affluent Americans but with what we had, we were the richest people on the planet. We had the music and, truly, we had it all.

Jammin' on the Rooftop - 1945
That's Stan on Tenor Sax and Phil Brenner on Trumpet

The "Riddle" Of Sinatra

Frank Sinatra, as we all know, produced some legendary records, but, the legend is more than a voice. The Axel Stordahl years in the late forties gave us the ultra romantic Sinatra after the Tommy Dorsey experience in the early forties.

Frank knew Nelson Riddle during those years when Riddle played trombone with Dorsey. When Frank brought in Nelson as an arranger and recorded on Capital in the fifties, they formed an ideal union. It was the marriage of a wonderful maturing voice set to some fantastic arrangements.

Frank made some great albums with Count Basie, Billy May, and others, but, the Riddle touch produced classics like Cole Porter's "Under My Skin," Jerome Kern's "The Way You Look Tonight," with a Dorothy Fields lyric, and the Gershwins' "Love Walked In." Those three tracks do it for me. They are basically lovely ballads framed by an upbeat tempo where voice and instruments blend perfectly. The Riddle touch was the deft and original use of Piccolos, Trombones, French Horns, and Strings. Those tracks represented a release for Frank from the straight slow ballads to which we danced the fox trot too many years ago. These records gave us the additional joy of dancing a slow lindy hop or just for pure listening enlightenment.

As an example, "I've Got You Under My Skin" begins with a soft relaxing beat that sensibly sets the tone and has become as familiar as the first few notes of Miller's "In The Mood," or Shaw's "Begin The Beguine." The mood is enhanced when Frank does a first chorus with phrasing that is delicious. But Riddle shows his own colors with a driving second chorus and a full band release featuring a wailing trombone that threatens to be a wild Basie-like finish. The ending however is a sudden return to that smooth enticing tempo just as the piece began. It is three minutes of genius that these two artists repeated in the other two tunes.

Torme

It was backstage at the Brooklyn Academy of Music around 1980 where Mel Torme had just given a concert. He was pleasant and articulate and still not satisfied with his limited success. My late wife Barbara, and I were guests of a friend who owned a record company and Mel talked like he hadn't really made it. To me he had made it big artistically, if not commercially.

Then in 1982 Concord Jazz Records produced a series of albums and he was reestablished as a prominent musical spokesman for Fred Astaire, Benny Goodman, and the Gershwins. Mel was an original... a vocal technician with perfect pitch and a unique style that ranged from pop crooning as in "Blue Moon" to the scat improvisations of "Lulu's Back In Town." I can recall an early Torme record called "County Fair" which was a combination of pop ballad, jazz, and light country. It made a distinct impression on me.

His virtuosity extended to songwriting having written "Lament To Love" for the Harry James Band when he was 16. Of course his big hit was "The Christmas Song" with lyrics by Bob Wells. He was a singer, drummer, and arranger as a teenager touring with a band led by Chico Marx of the famous brothers.

As an author in 1970, he wrote the *Other Side Of The Rainbow*, relating his frustrating experiences with the Judy Garland TV show in the sixties. He also penned a novel called *Wynner* in 1978 and an autobiography, *It Wasn't All Velvet* in 1988. Pretty good for a poor kid from Chicago. Mel Torme grew up in show business as a child actor with the Judy Garland - Mickey Rooney movies. I saw him in San Francisco with George Shearing and both were obviously having a good time on stage. On hearing of Mel's death Shearing said: "It is impossible to imagine a more compatible musical partner."

On the personal side, Mel was married four times, had five children, plus two adopted children, had affairs with Ava Gardner and Marilyn Monroe and had Buddy Rich as a lifelong friend. Based on his early crooning style, Fred Robbins, a New York DJ, nicknamed Mel "The Velvet Fog." Mel hated that tag.

A recent TV show featured some intricate medleys of Mel stringing together fragments of several standard tunes, sitting on drums for a Benny Goodman "Sing Sing Sing" solo, and a scat singing demonstration that could only be matched by Ella Fitzgerald. He virtually exploded with musical energy. As a realist he was one of the first to predict that the Big Band era as we knew it was dead and dying.

COMPOSERS

Harry's Mass

Harry Warren won 3 Academy Awards, was nominated for 8 others, had more songs on the Hit Parade than Irving Berlin, and between 1932 and 1957 wrote music for more musical films than any other composer.

His songs included standards like "42nd Street," "Lullaby of Broadway," "I Only Have Eyes For You," "Chattanooga Choo Choo," "Jeepers Creepers," "You Must Have Been A Beautiful Baby," "There Will Never Be Another You," "Nagasaki," "That's Amore," "I Found A Million Dollar Baby," "Cheerful Little Earful," "Atchison Topeka and S. F.," etc.

Hoagy Carmichael wrote "Star Dust" and Jerome Kern wrote "Ol' Man River." Yet "Atchison Topeka and S. F." is remembered as a Johnny Mercer tune. Johnny only wrote the lyric. Harry Warren wrote the music.

Harry came to Hollywood in 1929 and stayed on. He worked for all the major studios and wrote songs for 81 movies, including the theme from *Marty, An Affair To Remember*, and *Separate Tables*.

Warren grew up in Brooklyn Heights, played drums in a dance Hall in Canarsie, sold fruit at a

Yiddish Theatre in Brownsville, and worked as a stagehand. He played piano in silent movies, did a stint in the U S Navy, and then worked as a song plugger before starting to write his own songs.

He worked with Ira Gershwin in 1948 on the score for *The Barkleys of Broadway*. It was the last movie Fred and Ginger did together.

His name was Salvatore Guaragno but since he spoke Yiddish, most people thought he was Jewish.

From 1979 to 1981 his songs were cataloged by Michael Feinstein in California who spent his mornings working with Harry and his afternoons doing the same thing for Ira Gershwin.

Harry Warren wrote ballads, blues, dance tunes, waltzes, polkas, novelties and even TV themes (Wyatt Earp.)

He wrote a waltz that sounded like Debussy, wrote a complete mass and peformed it as "Harry's Mass" at Loyola Marymount College.

David Merrick, the crafty Broadway producer, bought the rights to *42nd St* from Warner Bros. He never mentioned it as Harry Warren's music. It was billed as David Merrick's Song and Dance Extravaganza. Harry Warren's name was never mentioned on the billing or on the original cast recording.

He helped Johnny Mercer write the music for "I'm An Old Cowhand" but refused to take credit for it. After the film came out with Crosby making it a big hit... it was too late.

He wrote mainly with Al Dubin who was 6 foot 3 and over 300 pounds. Dubin loved to eat, drank, did drugs, and was a frequent womanizer. Harry never knew where Dubin was but Dubin would write a lyric on a napkin or a greasy menu and once called Harry from a brothel in Mexico City with a lyric.

Harry Warren returned to Broadway to write a show called *Shangri-La* which was a complete flop. It had a good score and a cast with Dennis King, Martyn Green, and Carole Lawrence. Lines were flubbed, sets collapsed, and it opened during a June heat wave.

Harry's life was jinxed. He had a bad marriage, his son had died at 19, he had few friends, and he hated California. He never got the recognition partly because film songs are not usually associated with composers, unlike Broadway songs. Moreover, he never rubbed elbows with producers or went to Hollywood parties. He never advertised his songs in trade journals like other composers did. At one Academy Award dinner, he had to fight his way past the guards because he was not recognized even wearing a tuxedo.

Harry Warren had a good sense of humor. He once said that "song writers are lousy pianists. Irving Berlin plays with one finger, Jerome Kern plays with two fingers and I play with three."

The Sounds Of
Richard Rodgers

Richard Rodgers was born into the world of Franz Lehar and Jerome Kern and refused to follow his older brother and father into the medical profession. He was fortunate to have met Lorenz Hart and together they cemented a wonderfully productive working relationship — a collaboration that gave us more than 30 Broadway and West End shows, such as *Pal Joey* and *Babes in Arms*. After Hart's excessive drinking and unreliability became a problem, Rodgers achieved a triumphant second collaboration with Oscar Hammerstein. This union produced shows that were seen as the ultimate flowering of the musical theatre, with *Oklahoma*, *Carousel*, *South Pacific*, *The King and I* and *The Sound of Music* becoming household words.

These shows brought us the successful integration of the book, music, and lyrics that Rodgers had sought with Hart.

After the death of Hammerstein, Rodgers had his own problems with alcohol and writing shows with other lyricists even trying his own hand at lyrics. He was married for 49 years to Dorothy Feiner and they had 2 daughters, Mary and Linda. Both were talented and Mary wrote a successful off Broadway piece called *Once upon a Mattress*. Rodgers was so intricately involved in his music that he often neglected his family demonstrating a mean streak in his later years.

According to the critic-composer Alec Wilder, "there is an extraordinary incidence of inventiveness in practically all of Rodgers' songs... and they show the highest degree of consistent excellence... and sophistication." Though he wrote great music with Oscar Hammerstein, his greatest invention and freshness occurred during his younger years with Larry Hart.

Their first song was published in 1919 called "Any Old Place With You" when he was a mere 16. The pair really were put on the musical map when in 1925 they wrote The *Garrick Gaieties* with the hit song "Mountain Greenery." Although Rodgers wrote some film music, notably for *State Fair*, with Hammerstein, he was not happy with Hollywood and preferred writing for the stage. In his work with Hammerstein, he wrote some great songs but the flare that existed with Hart was missing. "It Might As Well Be Spring" was an exception with Hammerstein's superbly poetic lyric and a perfect matching melody that made this song a classic. Rodgers was usually very protective of how his songs were played and sung. When his lovely waltz, "Lover," was recorded by Peggy Lee in an up tempo, he was said to exclaim: "Why did Peggy pick on me. She could have killed "Silent Night."

Composers

But no composer could touch Rodgers for waltzes. Some of his best known were: "The Most Beautiful Girl In The World," "Carousel Waltz," "Wait Till You See Her," and "Many A New Day." Legend has it that among all the TV and radio stations in America and probably in the world, a Rodgers song may be heard at any time of the day or night all year round.

Irving Berlin, Always

There is a famous quote by Jerome Kern who said that "Irving Berlin has no place in American music. Irving Berlin IS American music."

Having written about 1500 songs, playing piano in only one key, unschooled, never learned to read music, he nevertheless was a rags to riches success and captured the pulse of America through two world wars. He wrote "White Christmas" and "Easter Parade"celebrating America's Christian holidays, wrote "There's No Business Like Show Business," which became a virtual theme song of the entertainment business. Sensing that there were too many patriotic songs being written for World War I, he put one back in his trunk. He retrieved it in 1938 for Kate Smith. "God Bless America", a virtual anthem, is not only a song but we find the words today on bumper stickers and windows all over America.

In 1911 he penned "Alexander's Ragtime Band," which was not a ragtime tune but it became his first big hit making him a key figure in American music. In 1918 he wrote an Army show called *Yip Yip Yaphank* with the unforgettable "Oh

How I Hate to Get Up in the Morning." He followed this in World War II with *This Is The Army* with all proceeds going to the Girl Scouts of America. He glorified the American girl in 1919 with "A Pretty Girl is Just Like a Melody." He set up his own publishing company, built his own theatre (The Music Box), and was a major songwriter for films and for the stage.

In the thirties he turned out hit dance songs for Fred Astaire starting with the the movie, *Follow The Fleet*. The songs kept America dancing with "Let Yourself Go," "Let's Face the Music and Dance," Cheek to Cheek," "Top Hat White Tie and Tails," and "Puttin on the Ritz."

His personal life in the early years was a struggle. He married Dorothy Goetz in 1913, a sister of Ray Goetz, the songwriter. On their honeymoon in Cuba, she became ill and died. On his return he wrote the beautiful, "When I Lost You." He married Ellin Mackay, the daughter of Clarence Mackay, founder of Postal Telegraph, over the objection of her family. His wedding present to her was the unforgettable "Always." During the depression it was rumored that Berlin rescued his father-in-law with a loan of one million dollars. It was a good story but probably not true. Other songs written for Ellin were "What'll I Do," "All Alone," and "Remember."

To those who doubted Irving Berlin's lyrical agility, consider these lines: "Before the fiddlers have fled, before they ask us to pay the bill and while we still have the chance, let's face the music and dance." These and other lines rival anything

Ira Gershwin could fabricate. Probably his finest show was *Annie Get Your Gun*. When it was just an idea that Rodgers and Hammerstein were producing and Dorothy Fields was writing the book, the music was to be composed by Jerome Kern. Tragically Kern died of a heart attack on a New York street. Rodgers and Hammerstein were able to convince Berlin to write the score and lyrics. So, ironically, Irving Berlin replaced the man who paid him his greatest tribute. Thus he was able to write the best show of his life.

Cole Porter – Mr. Sophistication

Cole Porter was born in Peru, Indiana but he found his natural home in Paris, a Venetian palazzo, or the French Riviera. That was his playground where he mingled with the rich and wrote sophisticated lines like "You're the nimble tread, of the feet of Fred Astaire" and topped it off with "You're Camembert." Or consider Finnan Haddie paired with my heart belongs to daddy. Porter wrote dazzling list songs like "You're The Top" and highly melodic tunes in minor keys with a preference for the beguine beat, like "Were Thine That Special Face" or "Love For Sale," Ironically his music grades at Yale were not that great with four D's, two C's, and two B's in music courses. However he developed an admiration for Homer and the Greek poets. He was also an admirer of the poems of Robert Browning.

With his grandfather's funds and his mother's encouragement of his musical training he attended Yale and Harvard where his cronies were Monty Wooley, Archie MacLeish, and Gerald Murphy. Murphy's father owned Mark Cross and with his wife Sarah were Scott Fitzgerald's models in ~~The Sun~~ ~~Also Rises~~ *TENDER IS THE NIGHT*. They all played a role in Porter's theatrical career. Cole married Linda Lee Thomas in 1919 and they lived their lives as world travelers on one long pleasure trip. It was a marriage of convenience since Cole was homosexual and Linda was believed to be a lesbian. Yet they were extremely devoted to one another. Linda cared for him after his leg was amputated as the result of a horseback riding accident.

Meanwhile the songs and shows were presenting Cole Porter with international renown. From 1928 to 1936 his Broadway shows were: *Fifty Million Frenchmen, The New Yorkers, Gay Divorce, Anything Goes, Jubilee,* and *Red Hot and Blue.*

The hit songs from these shows were: "Let's Do It," "What Is This Thing Called Love," "You Do Something To Me," "Night And Day," "I Get A Kick Out Of You," "You're The Top," "Blow Gabriel Blow," "Begin The Beguine," "It's De Lovely," and a score of others.

The lyrics were worldly, witty, sometimes naughty and especially amusing to the international set led by Elsa Maxwell, one of Cole's special admirers. Other shows followed: *Leave It To Me, Something For The Boys, Mexican Hayride,* and finally *Kiss Me Kate* in 1948 which is probably his finest work. His films were also notable such as: *Born To Dance, Rosalie, Broadway Melody of 1940, You'll Never Get Rich, Something To Shout About,* and *The Pirate.* The film, *Night and Day* was ostensibly biographical starring a macho Cary Grant as a war hero and composer but was widely regarded in Porter's circles as a joke.

His final work was in 1956 for the film *High Society*, a highly successful vehicle for Crosby and Sinatra. Cole Porter spent his last years living an opulent life at New York's Waldorf Astoria Towers furnished in splendor with a piano that was worth a fortune.

George and Ira Gershwin - Here To Stay

George Gershwin was always searching for something deeper musically and more formal, something grander. And he was able to write some serious pieces like "Opera Ala Afro-American" which was dropped from *George White's Scandals of 1922*. He wrote "Rhapsody in Blue" in 1924, "Piano Concerto" in 1925, and finally *Porgy and Bess* in 1935. While this development as a formal composer was going on, George Gershwin was writing some of the finest popular and theatre songs of the 30s and 40s.

And they were simple melodies... with a jazz and negro influence but less complex as he grew and became successful. The bulk of the songs were in the conventional AABA pattern. His songs were admired by jazz musicians as well as the dance bands and plugged considerably by the development of radio.

Lots of the Gershwin songs were written during the depression... but were not sad songs. They were uplifting tunes that were well received by a nation that needed a lift or a cheery sound. Even in his first published song with the unlikely title:

"When you want 'em you can't get 'em; When you've got 'em you don't want 'em"... he showed signs of originality and an effort to break away from the pattern of the average tunesmith.

He had his first big hit in 1919 with the ever popular "Swanee" which got a big boost from Al Jolson. For the *Scandals of 1922* he wrote "I'll Build a Stairway to Paradise" which marks the beginning of his theatrical career. In 1924 he wrote, "Somebody Loves Me," a tune that became a favorite of the jazz man that ranks with "How High The Moon" in jazz circles. Gershwin's "The Man I Love" written in 1924 had an interesting life. Originally in the show, *Lady Be Good* for Adele Astaire, it was removed after one week. Sometime later, Lady Mountbatten heard it, liked it and took it home to London to a dance band. It spread to Paris, finally in 1927 it was put into *Strike Up The Band*. The show closed after a short run. Flo Ziegfeld used it in "Rosalie" with the title "The Girl I Love." Ira Gershwin rewrote it, gave it to Helen Morgan to sing and it became the pop song that it is today. The lyric and melody are deceptively simple.

The Gershwins worked smoothly on their tunes. Gershwin was not addicted to the over-sentimental ballads as was his idol, Jerome Kern. And certainly, Ira, the professional wordsmith felt apathetic to a sentimental lyric. However in "Love Walked In" they achieved that harmony and cohesion on a slow song. The lyric is as pure and simple as the melody even though Ira felt it was "too churchy."

"Love Walked In" was the last song they completed together. "Our Love is Here to Stay" was the last but the tune had to be completed by Vernon Duke. The Gershwin songs that probably receive the most performances and requests are: "Embraceable You" and "The Man I Love." But there are dozens if not hundreds of Gershwin songs just as good.

Harold Arlen... Wherever The 4 Winds Blow

The giants of the American popular song are widely considered to be: Berlin, Gershwin, Kern, Porter, and Rodgers... in alphabetical order. And yet, these five giants all agreed that Harold Arlen should be among them. So let's put Harold Arlen up there in the top slot alphabetically and some critics seem to think he belongs there musically as well because of his versatility as a composer of every type of popular song whether written for Broadway, Hollywood, or whatever.

Among his peers he was highly regarded. Berlin and Kern came earlier and you might say they laid the groundwork for the others having labored in the vineyards of their European heritage, through the ragtime era, and Tin Pan Alley. Arlen came later but broke in as a singer, then as an orchestrator, and finally as a composer of popular songs. Like Berlin, his father was a cantor who improvised in many of his sermons. And Harold had the melodic and improvisational gifts that were conceivably inherited. He was on intimate terms with the jazz musician and his lonely world.

157

Indeed, the idea for "Sweet and Hot" a tune written in 1931 was from a hot lick Arlen heard from a trumpet player. If Woody Herman led the band that played the blues, Arlen was the guy who wrote the blues. But he did not confine himself to any type of song. He wrote ballads like "Last Night When We Were Young" an extraordinary composition with a fitting lyric by Yip Harburg; "My Shining Hour," almost a hymn, with a Mercer lyric; "Lets Fall In Love" with Ted Koehler; "This Time The Dream's On Me" a gem written with Johnny Mercer's lyric; novelty tunes like "Accentuate The Positive" also a Johnny Mercer lyric; jazz standards like "Get Happy" and "Only A Paper Moon"; words provided by Ted Koehler; and the definitive bar song "One For My Baby," a classic Sinatra piece, with Mercer setting the mood.

Hyman Arluck was born in Buffalo, made his mark composing for the Cotton Club productions in Harlem where he mingled with Cab Calloway, Duke Ellington, and Jimmie Lunceford then soared musically in New York and Hollywood. He worked with some of the finest lyricists of the day like E. Y. (Yip) Harburg, Ted Kohler, Ira Gershwin, Dorothy Fields, and of course, Johnny Mercer. Yet with all of these heavy hitters, his reputation reflected a mere shadow of his contemporaries who were knocking out long run shows like *South Pacific, Kiss Me Kate, Annie Get Your Gun, Show Boat*, and *Of Thee I Sing*. One explanation is that he liked the laid back life in Hollywood with his beautiful but unstable wife, Anya. He stayed on turning out background movie music and occasionally visiting New York when something promising came up, or when Marlene Dietrich called. Dietrich was a close friend. He was a disciplined writer but not as commercial as the other giants. In the shows *House of Flowers, Jamaica,* and *Saratoga,* he was not afraid to be experimental which may account for the lack of hits evolving from these shows. Another reason was a weakness in the librettos. He was not the Broadway musical composer in the sense that Richard Rodgers was. Ironically, Rodgers felt that *House of Flowers* which Arlen wrote with Truman Capote was one of the finest theatre musicals. And Irving Berlin declared that Harold was the best of us all.

In spite of the absence of a blockbuster show, Harold Arlen is one of the most recorded of American songwriters with albums of his songs by Ella Fitzgerald, Rosemary Clooney, Barbara Streisand, Lee Wiley, Eileen Farrell, Peggy Lee, K. T. Sullivan and Judy Garland. Arlen wrote the music for Broadway shows like *Bloomer Girl,* with Harburg; *House of Flowers,* with Truman Capote; *Jamaica,* with Harburg; *Saratoga* and *St. Louis Woman* with Johnny Mercer. His movie music was heard in *Star Spangled Rhythm, A Star is Born, Cabin In The Sky, Up in Arms, The Sky s The Limit, Here Come the Waves,* and, oh yes, *The Wizard of Oz,* his most successful score... I still get gooseflesh whenever I hear "Over The Rainbow."

Of the recognized ten best American popular songs ever written, Arlen is the only composer with two entries: They are "Stormy Weather" written with Ted Kohler and "Blues In The Night" with words by Johnny Mercer.

Here's Johnny... "that Long Long Road"

Writing lyrics with legendary composers like Harold Arlen, Jerome Kern, Hoagy Carmichael, Henry Mancini, Richard Whiting, and Duke Ellington, Johnny Mercer turned out a slew of classic songs like: "Too Marvellous For Words," "Laura," "Dream," "Come Rain Or Come Shine," "One For My Baby," "Hooray For Hollywood," "My Shining Hour," "Jeepers Creepers," "Accentuate The Positive," "Skylark," as well as four Oscar winners: 1. "Atcheson, Topeka, And Santa Fe" (he loved trains), 1946, 2. "In The Cool Cool Cool Of The Evening," 1951, 3. "Moon River," 1961, and 4. "Days Of Wine And Roses," 1962.

His catalog included over 1000 songs. "Lazy Bones" was written in 20 minutes. Mercer was a triple threat. He wrote lyrics, music, ("Birth Of The Blues," "I'm An Old Cowhand,' "The Waiter And The Porter") performed with Bing Crosby, Paul Whiteman, Jo Stafford, and Bobby Darin. As co-founder of Capital Records, he was a talent maker plugging Margaret Whiting, Peggy Lee, Nat King Cole, and Stan Kenton.

Johnny was born in Savannah, Georgia November 18, 1909, the son of a lawyer. He wanted to be an actor went to New York but instead became a songwriter. His first song was called "Out Of Breath And Scared To Death Of You" written in 1930 for *Garrick Gaieties*. He had his own radio show in 1942, and managed to write four Broadway shows, but only *Lil Abner* (1956) had any degree of success lasting 693 performances. His biography, called *My Huckleberry Friend* was written by his wife, Ginger. It might be out of print but his songs and words are still very much alive. He was affectionately called "everybody's lyric boy."

Royalty — The Duke

Was Duke Ellington a composer, a band leader, an arranger, or a pianist?? Of course, he was all of the above and superb in each category. He led one of the earliest of the Big Bands having grown up in Washington D. C. He and his band landed in Harlem's Cotton Club in 1927 and he augmented his band with musicians who were destined to be legendary in their own right. They included Johnny Hodges, Harry Carney, Bubber Miley, Cootie Williams, Rex Stewart, et al.

He wrote his share of songs, many of them standards like "Mood Indigo" and "I Let A Song Go Out Of My Heart." But his method was unlike most composers. Ellington used his orchestra as an instrument and the tunes were written for the instruments. Not content to write only songs, he composed a 50-minute suite called "Black, Brown, and Beige" and an extended piece called "Night Creature." Typical of his unique big band sound was a piece called "Rockin' In Rhythm" with a sound as distinctive and recognizable as a Miller sax section. In 1939 the brilliant arranger Billy Strayhorn joined the organization and together they turned out instrumentals with words added much later. Johnny Mercer put his lyrical touch to "Satin Doll" and Mitchell Parish wrote words to "Sophisticated Lady" (Ben Webster's big tenor sax practically made the tune his own.) Strayhorn was credited with "Lush Life" and the band's theme, "Take The A Train." Memorable, too, was the Hodges treatment on "Warm Valley" and dozens of others where Johnny Hodges exhibited the definitive alto sax.

Duke was able to keep his large well-paid band together through all the post-war slow times unlike most of the other bands. He carried on through the seventies always with new side men. He died in 1974 just shy of his 75th birthday. His multi musical talents will never be duplicated.

ESSAYS

That's What Friends Are For

The incident, as reported in all the papers, was the senseless shooting of a teacher in a Lake Worth, Florida Middle School hallway. What was not reported was the touching eulogy delivered at Barry Grunow's funeral. How does a person feel when a best friend is shot and killed? Mitch Krolick knows the agonized feeling.

When Barry's life was shortened by a student's gun, Mitch was stunned. They had been basketball buddies, you might say, getting together each Sunday for a weekly workout and then would debate the relative merits of the Detroit Pistons and the New York Knicks. You see, Barry was from Monroe, Michigan; Mitch from New York. Ordinarily the combination, to sport fans, is like oil and water, but, not for these two.

It was not unusual, therefore, for Mitch to give a eulogy for his friend, Barry. BUT THIS WAS NOT YOUR RUN OF THE MILL EULOGY. Mitch prefaced it with some basketball references about their games and debates and then suddenly told the

166

hushed crowd to bear with him a moment. Mitch stepped back and produced a basketball, then proceeded to remove his jacket and slipped on a DETROIT PISTON's jersey. To a surprised audience he continued with the following words holding the ball against his chest:

"It is my honor today to be asked to speak about someone whom I considered a great man. I knew Barry for about nineteen years having met him while we were both employees at a music store in North Palm Beach..."

"Through the years I became close to his family, enjoying two Thanksgiving meals each year, one with my family and one with his... For Barry and I, playing in basketball leagues and flag football leagues was as commonplace as going to work and a lot more enjoyable. I remember how excited he was about the prospect of teaching in the Palm Beach County School System. He always said that he was going to make a difference in his classes... Anyone could tell that teaching was Barry's niche. He played by the rules but found ways to bend them to make his classes more fun and more interesting....

"The wedding of Pam and Barry was a blast. I was the DJ. When it came time to feed the wedding cake to each other, they smashed me with the cake rather than themselves. Talk about a sense of humor.... Barry brought the same passion he had for sports and teaching to parenting. He truly enjoyed his young family - Sam and Lee-Anne.... It was a real tragedy and he will be sorely missed by all those with whom he came into contact."

Looking up toward the sky and pointing to the jersey on his chest, Mitch said: "Well, Barry, what do you think?" Mitch continued: "I'll never forget you, Barry. I know you can hear me." The words gave quite a lift to the room full of teary-eyed relatives and friends. A few misunderstood the scene with the ball and jersey and thought it was rather juvenile. When Mitch was asked how he felt after delivering this speech about the death of his dear friend, he replied calmly, "That's what friends are for."

Is A Rose Still A Rose?

In leafing through a magazine recently in a doctor's office, I came across a listing of musical groups playing gigs in the New York City area. I realize that popular music has undergone some heavy changes, that the so-called elevator music or jazz as I knew it are old hat. Yet I continue to be amazed and amused at the creative variety as well as the crude audacity of names applied to musical groups. Nowhere, in most cases, is there an identifying clue or hint of a musical aggregation. In the prehistoric days of the big bands, there was Les Brown and His Band of Renown, and Tommy Dorsey, the Sentimental Gentlemen of Swing, or Artie Shaw, the King of the Clarinet, or even Guy Lombardo with his Sweetest Music This Side of Heaven. We knew in those days what we were in for. These were unquestionably musicians playing popular music, sometimes jazz, sometimes swing, and sometimes sweet.

But fast forward and today we have Super Furry Animals, a British group with a name, I believe, that has no relation to the type of music being conveyed, if it's music at all. Or consider

Those Bastard Souls, which might reveal a certain aspect of birth, but, hardly a description of its music. Then there is Mike Viola and the Candy Butchers. Do you listen to them, look at them, or lick them? How about Saltine? This must be a group one takes with soup. Another band is called Aluminum Group which I would expect to find in a catalog of metalurgists and certainly not in a directory of Local 802 musicians.

What would you expect to hear from Sparklehorse? This one might look good in the fourth at Belmont. And the Swinging Neckbreakers, if taken literally, would produce visions of gymnastic hammer holders rather than elastic legged guitar slingers. The Zen Guerillas, if not found caged in a zoo, would most likely be sought as a pseudo-religious organization. I had just about adjusted to the inevitability of The Grateful Dead, The Who, The Monkeys, and Jefferson Airplane but the new names have me baffled. What they spew out to their hordes of followers is one thing, but, what they call themselves is an exercise in barbaric nomenclature.

The next time you feel like going out on a Saturday night for entertainment, you have all of these to choose from: The Black Halos; The Go; The Funky Meters; Man or Astroman?; Bottle Rockets; etc. etc. etc.

A Little Girl Raised Her Hand...

"Why don't YOU run for office?" And with these words from a sixth grade student, Tierney Cahill faced a unique challenge as a teacher. It was during a history lesson on ancient Greece at Reno, Nevada's Sarah Winnemucca Elementary School. It was September, 1999 and as Tierney told it, "I went into the differences between America's representative democracy and the Greek model of direct democracy. I began to talk about the great Athenian general, Pericles, and explained that he felt that if you don't participate in your democracy you have no place in society." At that point, a little girl raised her hand and said: "Well, that may have been fine for the Greeks, Ms. Cahill, but you can't run for office in this country unless you are a millionaire or unless you know a lot of them." Tierney mulled this over. Wow, she's already figured that out. But being a positive and optimistic teacher, Tierney replied, "That's not exactly true; all citizens in our country have the right to run for office." The little girl, without batting an eyelash, shot right back with. "Well then why don t you prove it, Ms. Cahill, and why don't YOU run for office.You ll be great. You're funny and fair."

Tierney was in shock. She thought, what have I gotten myself into? I wanted to say, who me? No way. I'm a divorced single mom with three little kids of my own (ten, seven, and six.) There's just no possible way I could do this. Tierney paused, took a deep breath, looked at that little girl's face and then at the class where suddenly "all eyes were peering at me anticipating a response." I realized that we ask children to be brave all of the time. We ask them to be leaders, say no to peer pressure, turn down drugs, step away from the crowd and not be afraid to take on challenges. But how often do they see anyone do that? How often are they told that "you CAN do and be anything you want to be in life?" Finally, completely terrified, Tierney told the kids that she had to sleep on it and she would give them an answer the next day.

There was no sleep that night. Tierney was 33, had been teaching eleven years, had taught high school social studies and had owned a pre-school for three years. She had never been confronted by anything like this. The more she thought about it, the more it seemed that it was an omen, a premonition, something she might have to do. The next morning, she met with her Principal, Vice Principal, and Assistant Superintendent and received a qualified go. However, no grades could be connected to the project, no school materials could be used, and she would need signed waivers from parents for each child to participate.

Tierney told the class she WOULD run for office providing that they got involved in the process. "Of course they wanted me to run for President, but, I'm too young." However when it was learned that Jim Gibbons, the Republican Congressman in her district ran unopposed in the last election and was running unopposed again, Tierney could step into the void. Some void. There hadn't been a Democrat elected from her district in decades. Still it was like the Red Sea being parted and nothing stood in her way. The Democratic Party approved of her candidacy but its participation was unenthusiastic. There was some lip service, a few invitations to speak, curiosity but little real support like funds.

The real support came from her students who designed logos and flyers, walked precincts, put up signs, and virtually ran her campaign. And the focus was on — THE PROCESS. The issues of gun control and campaign financing were secondary. The issue of women in politics was only incidental. Northern Nevada was cow country where both parties opposed gun control. Tierney stressed THE PROCESS. The children would learn how our officials are elected and serve and represent their constituencies. That would be a valuable lesson.

It was hard work. There were nights when Tierney's own children did their homework in the back of a union hall and passed out campaign buttons and literature at the end of the meetings. Some of the parents helped with moral support. Tierney's principal was reluctantly behind the effort, fearful of consequences that would be detrimental to the school system. Tierney's own family helped by posting signs all around town.

She was expected to get no more than ten percent of the vote and though her campaign war chest was a mere $7,000, she actually garnered 34%... and that was without a recount. John Porter who ran in a neighboring district had almost one million dollars to draw on but drew only 89,500 votes compared with Tierney's 106,000.

When asked if she was ever interested in politics, Tierney replied, "Being an Irish Catholic Democrat, public service was drilled into our dear little heads from early on. If you didn t become a nun, the next best thing was to marry a Kennedy or at the very least, become a teacher." In retrospect, it was a wonderful experience. The Democratic Party could have done a lot more but her candidacy seemed fruitless and they respectfully backed off. Tierney had a number of endorsements. The NEA (National Education Association) endorsed her and sent her a check for $1,000. The AFL-CIO endorsed her but sent no money. "I received a check of $130 from the WUFPAC (Women Under Forty Political Action Committee.) In June of 2000 I was invited to speak to the Red Rock Democratic Club in Las Vegas and met some of the party powers. They seemed polite about my 'little class project' but no offers to help in any way. When Al Gore was invited to Las Vegas to accept the Teamster's endorsement, I was not invited. Likewise when Joe Lieberman made his appearance. In the last couple of days before the election I was booked to make so many local speeches and appearances running around like a maniac in the evenings and teaching full time that I rarely slept." When the results came in Tierney was suddenly seen as a Democratic darling, an upcoming force by the party heads in the State. She didn't believe them. Tierney Cahill may have lost the election but facing up to that student's challenge was a personal triumph. Her campaign was a spectacular win for her students. And her noble performance didn't exactly hurt the teaching profession.

One More Kick

Friends come in all sizes. Some folks like them with four legs. I had one with four wheels. I was never disappointed. Mine was as faithful as a Labrador Retriever and it purred like a kitten for the two years in my possession.

Our relationship began on a sunny day in May of 1995 outside a Florida Cadillac showroom. It had a desert white tinge with a rag top of beige. It glittered with a discreet radiance but seemed anxious to get on the road, to strut its stuff. The tires had a white streak in lieu of the outdated white walls, the chrome glistened in the bright sunshine. Yet, it was not flashy or brassy or as low slung as some of those sporty cars. It had all the technical and electronic advances from adjustable seat positions, to recording outside temperatures. I couldn't have cared less if it showed me temperatures in Taiwan. It was just a solid lithe dependable body. When I kicked those tires, it never flinched.

It was mine for 24 months or 30,000 miles, whichever came first. I can remember the first trip. We planned to stay with some friends in New York City. On the trip up from Florida that 200 plus horsepower engine responded to my slightest touch as I put it through its paces. It never uttered a sound above that soothing purr, as comfortable as watching a movie at Radio City Music Hall.

I parked it in a narrow yard beside the two story house where our friends said it would be safe. Everyone admired it for its size and interior space. It had a stately posture and I felt as proud as a papa. When it was time to return home I grew a little careless and in backing out of that spot I scraped the rear fender. I was near tears. I rushed it to a nearby body shop and two hours later it looked as good as new. The repair man was as deft as a plastic surgeon.

There were other trips in and around Florida and my four wheeled pet behaved impeccably. It was grace under pressure. I brought it in for regular checkups, cleaned it inside and outside incessantly, with my own hands, not trusting it to those instant electronic car washes. For 25,000 miles I treated it like a baby except when I drove over a road barrier one dark night or hit the sidewalk curb when negotiating a sharp right turn. It might have been hurt but it didn't complain... never.

And it didn't matter whether it was born in Japan or Jakarta. I was aware of its rich heritage dating back to 1910 when the first closed bodies were built as standard equipment. But you can't hold back time and the inevitable moment came. I said my fond goodbye in the comfort that someone else would continue the pleasure, that the wheels would continue to turn in rain or shine. In a final expression of gratitude and emotion I looked down at the tires and gave it one more kick.

Babe Ruth's Unbroken Record

By Norman Krolick as told to Stan Krolick

Baseball records are made to be broken. Luis Castillo believed that, when he threatened recently to topple Joe DiMaggio's unbelievable 56 game hitting streak. However, Luis was thwarted at a mere 35. It reminded me that the most famous baseball record was Babe Ruth's 60 home runs in one season, which held up as something sacred for almost 70 years. And I remember my brother Norm's story of the Babe which he loved to tell and retell. Yet it had nothing to do with his home run record or his baseball ability.

"It was the early 1930's in the Bronx when as a teenager I held the enviable position of a Western Union messenger. This was complete with uniform, spats, and a commission of pennies for every wire delivered or solicited. I had to supply my own bicycle, of course, which was purchased used and a bit rickety to say the least. I was assigned a territory that included the Yankee Stadium. When there weren't any messages to deliver,

I had to solicit people who might want to send holiday greetings for Christmas, New Year's, etc.

"One morning in May, with no telegrams to deliver and while canvassing the area for Mother's Day greetings, I wandered by the Stadium where the Yankees were scheduled to play the Boston Red Sox. Usually there was a guard at the gate near the players' entrance. On this day, however, it was either too early or too late and no one was at the gate. I couldn't believe it.

"Naturally I went in thinking I could sell a few telegrams to the players, most of whom were not from New York, and who might wish to send a Mother's Day message back home. As I entered the locker room the first person I spotted was unmistakably Babe Ruth. He had taken off his shirt getting ready to don his uniform. I was quite surprised at his impressive physique having seen him only in pictures. The Babe greeted me with, "Hi, Kid, what's on your mind?" Overcoming my excitement in the presence of greatness, I blurted out my Mother's Day mission. The Babe said, "Well, kid, if I had a mother I'd surely send her a message. But here's a dollar bill. Send your own mother a telegram."

"I was shocked. I don't know whether it was the money he gave me or just going face to face with someone who was already a living legend. Then to my further amazement, he went to each of his teammates who were there and collected a dollar from Lou Gehrig, Earl Combs, and many of those Yankee greats and presented me with a handful of bills. In the depression years, a dollar was like gold. I barely had the sense to mutter, "Thanks, Mr. Ruth," and I scampered out thinking it was a dream.

"Looking back at this incident, I recognize that over the years I have earned a lot more than I received that day. But, nothing could have been more satisfying. It was one of the most memorable days of my life and nourished my hero worship for many years. It was just another typical Babe Ruth story. But this one happened to me. Although his home run record was finally broken, his record for generosity, in my estimation, was unbreakable."

This story originally appeared in the HAPPY TIMES MONTHLY, 2002, Boca Raton, FL

A Tear For Jakey

I have never owned a dog. I never wanted one. The nearest thing to a pet I ever had was a gold fish and that wasn't much fun. Dogs were just not part of my life or my family history. As a result I never had much love or affection for any of them or even took an interest in other people's dogs.

While their owners would carry on about them, kiss them, talk to them, or even sleep with them, it was something that was beyond my comprehension. One relative of mine loves his dog so much that his wife sits in the back of the car while his dog sits up front next to the driver's seat. Maybe it was some innate fear of animals or merely my own indifference, I just couldn't get too emotional about any dog I ever met... at least not until I met Jakey.

His name is Jake but everyone calls him Jakey. I couldn't really avoid him since he was so large - a black Labrador Retriever - who is owned by my nephew and niece Josh and Caren Bennett. Whenever my wife and I visited them, perhaps once a week, Jakey was there running up to everyone, sniffing and wagging his tail incessantly. He barks but never bites. He is gentle and harmless and loves the kids Sam and Marti. I grew to like him. And I think he knows me as another member of the family. Perhaps it is the bone I throw him whenever I come in and applaud when he catches it just before it hits the floor. Or maybe it is the table food I pass him under the table when we sit down to dinner. No one could be annoyed at Jakey. He is part and parcel of the family.

Recently Jakey was acting lethargic and was taken to the Vet for an examination. The diagnosis was guarded and we all held our breath. It was cancer but confined to one of his toes. He had to have the toe removed to avoid the cancer from spreading. I actually shed a tear for him. When the Vet expressed optimism that it wouldn't spread, we were all relieved. I saw Jakey a few weeks ago and the missing toe didn't seem to bother him. Like the comeback of Seabiscuit he was raring to go. He jumped for his bone with the same dexterity and as always, I applauded, and, like a dog lover, I spoke to him, and petted him, with an emotional intensity I had never shown before.

Letter From A Substitute Teacher

Dear Stan,

This is my third year as a substitute teacher in the Palm Beach School System. I was a young 74 in my first year of teaching. I had retired you know as an insurance agent and then as a Government employee and my grandchildren conned me into serving as a school aide so that I could see more of them. When a critical shortage of teachers occurred, the system sent out alarms for subs. With the only qualifications a bachelor's degree and a desire to work with kids, I decided to test the waters. I had never been on the teacher's side of a classroom before.

So there I was in a new career, my third, as nervous as a kid in his first day in first grade. It was little comfort that the principal offered me words of encouragement or that the permanent teacher would always leave a lesson plan for me. I still had to face those puzzled but unpredictable four and five year old faces peering at me. I sensed it at first as a conflict. After some moments that seemed like hours, I looked over the class and noticed some rumbling rising to a sound short of chaos. I announced my name and my purpose. They grew inquisitive and started a barrage of questions. "Why are you here? Where is our teacher? " And before it got out of hand, I roared, with all the authority of a policeman: "I must have absolute quiet." That worked with the four and five year olds.

Later when I subbed for an older group and they became unruly, I had to resort to sterner measures. I put my two fingers in my mouth and whistled like I used to do at football games. It worked like a charm and by the time the class had ended, they wanted to know how I did that and would I teach them the "finger whistle." Often when I seemed confused as to the next lesson or the next activity, the children knew better than I and in many respects I was dependent on them for directions, especially when it was lunch time.

I had some success during a social studies lesson in describing a recent trip to Alaska. The kids listened in awe as I told about bears I had seen in Juneau, the bald eagles in Sitka, and rafting down the rapids of the Mendenhall River.

It gradually dawned upon me that substitute teaching can be frustrating. There was only a lesson plan to follow and to control a class, establish rapport, and to actually start teaching a subject given the time limitations was almost impossible. Sometimes I considered myself a babysitter and counted the minutes to the bell. Yet the total experience was gratifying. For example, one day when the class was dismissed and the kids were getting on their busses, one little boy ran back into the room and shouted, "I forgot to say goodbye to you, Mr. Teacher." Moments like those cannot be measured in a paycheck. I found that teaching is more than a job. It is a grave responsibility and takes a lot of patience and caring. And incidentally, by subbing, I do see a lot more of my grandchildren.

As Ever,
Your Brother Bert

FICTION

The Race to Tasmania

The seas were choppy, the air was chilly, but in sweaters and jackets we sat bundled up on the promenade deck aboard the huge ocean liner bound for Australia. Before leaving Auckland, however, we were caught up in the excitement of Team New Zealand preparing to defend America's Cup, the yachting world's greatest prize. It was a major event in Auckland for the tiny country of New Zealand. It seemed like the entire population was down near the harbor to get a glance at the yachtsmen and the sailing vessels. The scene had all the hype and hoopla of a World Series game. As our cruise ship slipped out of its berth the traditional sailaway festivities commenced with drinks lined up on the top deck. The harbor was aglow in the bright afternoon sun with a flotilla of sail boats of all sizes.

A chap standing next to us on the railing was enthusiastic about seeing the great sailing ships screaming good luck to the New Zealand crews. "God would I like to sail on one of those ships. It must be a hoot to be one of the crew." He was blonde, exuberant, well built, in his late twenties, striking in a white sweat shirt with red and white stripes about the neck and blue shorts. "Well why haven't you done it? You look strong enough." "Tennis was my game until I tore up my knee. Then I did a little singing in San Francisco. I hear there's a great piano bar on this ship. I like to sit around a good piano player and sing the show tunes. Now I'm a computer programmer in Hawaii. Say, I'm George Barton. What's yours?" "Robert Kay. Call me, Bob. And this is my wife, Linda." "So, George, what brings you to this part of the world," chimed in my wife. "Just a vacation, with my partner, Brian, who must be under the table by now." "What is this America's Cup all about?" Linda inquired innocently. Linda was only trying to make conversation since I had already briefed her on this famous yachting event. George jumped at the bait, saying: "The regatta consists of nine races I believe spread over a couple of days. But the race is not all about sport, unfortunately. Like lots of sports these days, it's more about business and money. Backing and financing America's Cup are tycoons who may love sailing but they dream about winning and making money out of it. Fortunes have been won and lost in this sport. There's heavy backing this year for Team Switzerland to snare the Cup away from New Zealand, the defending champions. Isn't that ironic? Switzerland a land locked country with a yachting team?" "They do have amazing lakes, "countered Linda. After a few more drinks the harbor was fading from sight and the crowd on the deck seemed to disperse. "Why don't you and your companion join us for dinner,

George? I'll arrange it with the dining room staff for 8:30." "Sounds, swell, but I'll have to check with Brian... if I can find him. Bye for now." And he was off. "Nice kid, don't you agree, Linda?" "Yes, charming. Let's find a few chairs and breathe some good clean air."

So after sailaway my wife and I found ourselves cruising on the Tasman Sea in adjacent deck chairs being mesmerized by watching the swell of the waves. It had the same hypnotic force as staring at a roaring fireplace. When my wife got up and went back to the cabin, I sat alone then dozed a bit, read a bit, and dozed a bit more. When I awoke another passenger, a man, was seated on the deck chair that my wife had vacated.

As our eyes met he was smiling. "You kick up quite a storm, old chap." "I'm sorry. Was I snoring that loudly?" "Well, I would say to be kind, that it blended in quite nicely with the sound of the waves."

The formalities grew into some heavy talk about growing old and how I was trying to exercise, eat less, and how difficult it was to minimize food intake on a cruise ship. He was recalling happier days when he was thinner, spryer and before "the incident." At this point he lowered his head and said, "I would like to tell you a sad story." "Fire away," I said with my best listening antennae raised. His tale of woe was heart breaking but his face did not betray any genuine sadness. Apparently he had told the story so often that it was almost a routine. Often total strangers confide, total strangers become confidants and innocent sounding boards.

Without any further prompting on my part, other than a queer curiosity, he swept into the story of how he and his wife, both Australian, couldn't have children, finally adopting a baby boy. With a peculiar smile he said, "at the tender age of fourteen he was gone." Suddenly aroused, I sat up. "Gone? What do you mean gone?" "The lad took off without a clue and we haven't seen him since. An investigation turned up nothing." Letting me digest that for a minute, he took a breath and started to elaborate." Actually the five-year investigation did turn up something. It was something I never expected. It seems that the investigator on the case got so involved that he became more than a bit interested in my wife. It got to the point for me that I didn't realize which was the worst tragedy: my son's disappearance or losing my wife. Just then the Captain came on the speaker with the unexpected news that a fellow passenger "needed medical attention and we would be heading at top speed for the nearest hospital which was in Hobart, Tasmania, an island just off the coast of Australia. It meant that the ship would be bypassing Fiord National Park and the fantastic Milford, Doubtful, and Dusky Sounds, some of the most amazing scenic wonders and waterfalls in this part of the world. The Captain further explained that we would have to increase our speed to a maximum of 21 knots to get us to shore about twelve hours before scheduled. It would mean some discomfort on the ship and he cautioned us to be careful when walking and to use the hand-rails. He expressed his regret at this turn of events and felt that all passengers would understand.

I abruptly rose from my deck chair, excused myself to my new companion, saying that I had to get back to the cabin and to see my wife. "I hope we can continue our little talk later," I said, and left.

Rumors on the ship began to circulate like an epidemic and before long everyone I met had a different story about this medical emergency." Someone said, "it was just another terrorist threat." Rumors beget rumors. One passenger said that he had heard that a crewman had attacked a passenger. Another thought that a passenger had injured a crewman who was attacking her. Back in the cabin, with the ship starting to roll, I reviewed the tour book to assess what scenery we would be missing. One of my purposes of this trip was to witness the magnificent fiords and write an article as the ship would gracefully wind its way through the majestic natural sites. It was clear that I would have to reassess my literary intentions.

We dressed for dinner for the formal dining room as the ship pitched and rolled incessantly. In addition to the increased speed of the ship the seas were becoming more turbulent and more uncomfortable for all of the passengers. In spite of this, or maybe because of it, some guests at a table near us were trying to maintain a more frivolous mood. Obviously on a dare one woman climbed on top of her table and started drinking vodka shots to the applause and encouragement of her table mates. After about ten of these shots she was helped down and almost collapsed in her seat. Through all of this a piano player was doing the tunes from "Fiddler on the Roof." There were a few birthday celebrations with the dining room staff gathering to sing "Happy Birthday" in a variety of accents. Although we were seated at a table for four, our two guests were no-shows. Furthermore, our waiter had no knowledge of a cancellation. After dinner we carefully negotiated the length of the ship to the Show Lounge where we observed passengers clutching the hand rails or each other. It looked like a mass drinking orgy with everyone staggering. The show went on amid a blaze of lights and color. The singers and dancers on the stage performed seemingly oblivious to the ship's radical motion.

Onward to the casino and after a spell of blackjack, I decided to leave my wife at the crap table where she was doing quite well without my intervention. I sauntered down to the Purser's Desk which seemed to be unmanned. If anyone knew what was going on, I thought surely the Purser would know. I rang the bell and a young uniformed woman appeared with a name tag that read Jacqueline Greco, Malta. Having been to that tiny island only a few months ago, I mentioned that beautiful harbor and how much we had enjoyed being there. She said she was homesick and was on the verge of tears. When I asked what was the matter, she told me her dilemma.

"I am meeting my fiancé and my family in Sydney for a shipboard wedding and the Captain was to marry us. But I have been told that for security purposes the ship policy has been revised and visitors would not be permitted on the ship at Sydney."

I tried consoling her saying that "I'm sure it will all work out. And by the way I was overcharged at the Internet Café and would appreciate a credit. It seemed I couldn't get on line for about 15 minutes."

"Of course," she said. "I'll see that you will get a credit on your shipboard account. What is your cabin number?"

"6260, the name is Mr. And Mrs. Kay. And another thing. Were there any messages for me from a George Barton?"

"No, sir. I'm afraid not."

"Meanwhile, maybe you can tell me why the Captain is in such a rush to get to Hobart. Is there another reason?" Restoring her Purser's demeanor and wiping her eyes, she said that a young man was involved in an accident and there was a lot of bleeding. While he has been stabilized and the bleeding stopped, he will need the services of a doctor and a hospital environment.

"Can you tell me the man's name?"

"I don't know the man's name, Mr. Kay."

"Well, thank you, Jacqueline. I hope the lad pulls through and I trust you will be able to make alternate wedding plans."

Before returning to the cabin, I stopped off at the Piano Bar. There, Elaine Wood and her piano were encircled by her faithful fans doing some familiar bawdy tunes. It was apparent that George Barton was not in this lounge.

Returning to the cabin, my wife was jubilant about the fifty dollars she had won within twenty minutes but didn't think she could sleep with the sounds of all the deck chairs rumbling and the waves hitting the ship. The ship meanwhile had hit some rough weather and was being tossed around like a toy in a child's bathtub. "Just one night of this and we'll be ashore in the morning," I said. "Yes, and we'll all need a hospital when this night is over."

It was a difficult night, indeed, in spite of a few shots of scotch that I thought would lull me to sleep. It was amazing that an 80 thousand ton ship could be tossed around as if it was being tested. Shortly after midnight the Captain came on again to assure everyone that he was trying to divert the ship's course and bypassing the fiords." We would be in smooth seas within an hour," he added.

When we awoke the ship was docking amid a sea of sailing ships. We were in Hobart, Australia's second oldest city, rich in history, and in the shadow of Mount Wellington. The harbor was wide awake as we docked on a hot sunny day. There were ambulances waiting at dockside and at the gangplank a uniformed band with bagpipes were bellowing chorus after chorus of "Waltzing Mathilda." It was a curious sight to see this ailing young man being carried off the ship accompanied by the music of a bagpipe band. We decided to go ashore and explore the city of Hobart. The taxis were lined up waiting for passengers to disembark. We engaged a woman driver with long blonde hair wearing a black pants suit. She agreed to give us an overview of the city. It was good to get out of the hot sun into an air conditioned car.

The most popular site for tourists was the old jail where records were displayed of prisoners who were transported from England incarcerated for the slightest of crimes like stealing a loaf of bread or a bicycle or a pair of shoes, or merely panhandling. We were then taken to a shopping street which featured wooden carvings and local crafts and a whole room full of clocks. We purchased a small clock made from the wood of a sasafras tree.

Our guide then dropped us off at a local seafood restaurant called Kelly's near the harbor which she said was the best in town. A genial proprietor served us and guaranteed his fish was caught fresh daily and assured us we would love it. What we really loved was the pitcher of cold local beer he brought to the table before anything else. There were few customers in the restaurant now since it was late for lunch and we told him about the lad on the ship. He was not surprised. In fact he said "every time a liner hits this port there are ambulances waiting for sick passengers. I wonder what they feed people on those ships."

We walked back to the ship which was scheduled to leave at 3PM for Melbourne and then Sydney. The crew was not giving out any information other than the Captain will be in touch with all passengers. On the way back, my wife stopped to talk to another passenger. I ran into Jacqueline, the purser from Malta. She smiled when she recognized me.

"Hey Mr. Kay, what do you know," she said, happily, "I'm getting married at a church in Sydney and my family and fiancé will be there. Do you believe this?"

"That's great, Jacqueline. Very happy for you."

"And the reception will be at the Intercontinental Hotel with a honeymoon suite for two nights." The ship was to be berthed at Sydney for three days so she would be able to reboard the ship and continue the journey back to Auckland.

"And best of all, John is booking as a passenger for the remainder of the cruise.

"Well, congratulations," I said. "I told you it would all work out. By the way, what's the latest on the young man who was carried off the ship?"

"I hear that he was doing fine, and Oh yes. His name is George Barton."

"So what was the nature of his injury?"

"Well, you know he was sharing a cabin with his partner, and I suppose there was some aggressive activity... sexual, you know."

"Oh, I see." At this point I felt a little ashamed to have been so inquisitive. On board the ship the Captain announced that "the medical authorities had taken care of the situation and we sail at 1500 hours for Melbourne." The rest of the cruise was smooth sailing.

Johnny Got His Gig

The advertisement appeared in Variety, the famous theatrical publication. John Solo was in a mid-town New York City coffee shop having breakfast alone idly flipping the pages when he spied it: "WANTED: Handsome, dignified actor, over 65, no family ties, Shakespearean a plus, not susceptible to seasickness. Call 212-578-8076 for audition." It was strange, as he read and reread the Ad. He seemed to fit the bill having once done a Shakespeare festival in Lenox, Massachusetts. But the allusion to "seasickness" was puzzling. He called the number in the Ad more out of curiosity than genuine interest in the position. A woman answered and asked some fundamental questions about his age, experience, and "where can you be reached." She would not impart any further information and said "you'll be notified within two weeks." John walked away from the phone booth more interested and more confused than ever. He thought about it for the next few days and then seemed to let it pass from his mind. He was overly concerned about landing his next job in the theatre. The parts on Broadway for him were few and

Fiction

far between according to his agent. His age was his main enemy. Straight plays were scarce and he was tired of road shows and regional theatre.

It was in this depressed frame of mind that he came home to his apartment one day to find a message on his tape that said: "Please call 212-578-8075 for audition." He had almost forgotten about the mysterious Ad in Variety. He thought the taped message concerned a play being mounted at an Off Broadway theatre which he had discussed that afternoon with a director-friend. When he called and identified himself, the female voice advised him briskly to be at an office near Lincoln Center the very next day at 9AM sharp for an audition.

He appeared at the appointed time and place and was shown into a small unadorned office with a desk, chair, and side chair. At this point he remembered the Variety Ad but before he could say "What is this all about?" a tall stately gentlemen entered wearing a white shirt, tie, blue blazer, and grey trousers. "Good morning, John. I guess we owe you an explanation."

"Yes, I believe you do," John said.

At this point the man took out a booklet and asked him to read one page which "would explain everything". It read as follows:

"Certain special guests of LUXURY CRUISE LINES can enjoy the gracious attention of our acclaimed Social Hosts. These specially selected gentlemen are aboard our ships to complement and supplement the many functions of the cruise."

"They are aboard not as hired staff but as cruise enthusiasts to help guests enjoy their vacations to the limit. Easy conversationalists, these knights of the sea will accompany a specified guest or guests to dinner or social events or merely provide relaxed, comfortable conversation...."

"Now, Mr. Solo, my name is Ken and I am a travel agent representing LUXURY CRUISE LINES and I would like to know if you are willing to participate on a 60-day cruise as a companion to one of our very special guests."

"O.K." John blurted, "that explains the reference to seasickness... but what about the Shakespeare bit?"

"Well, John, the person who has requested this special companion would like a social host to read her passages from various Shakespeare plays each day. And not just to read but to act them out. The choice of plays will be yours. She has promised to reward you handsomely which would be in addition to the basic salary the cruise line is prepared to offer. The cruise line pays $3,000 for the cruise. She will add another $50,000 for the right actor." The mathematics seemed inviting and John asked

"When is the audition?"

"You have just had it, John, since you qualify, and there were no other respondents who filled the bill. The ship sails on June 5th from Pier 32. The name of the ship is *The Shining Sea*. She returns August 4th. There will be a few days of training and you'll need this manual. If you consent, the client would like to meet you tomorrow at this office, at the same time. There will be some paper work to fill out, of course. What do you say, John?"

"Who is this special lady, may I ask?"

"Her name is Elizabeth Van, a lady of wealth whose husband left her well endowed. She is 86, spry, a little eccentric, and loves Shakespeare. Will you accept, John?"

"It sounds like an interesting challenge. I'll brush up on my Shakespeare and be back tomorrow to meet Mrs. Van."

"Splendid."

Elizabeth Van was tired. She was tired of bankers, attorneys, accountants telling her how to invest, how to reduce her estate tax, how to spend her money. These professional money managers were engaged by her late husband in an effort to help her conserve her estate. Since she had no heirs, she saw no reason to conserve the estate.

Elizabeth Van had been an aspiring actress when her husband, a sometime producer of plays, met and married her, effectively removing her from the work force. There were no children. He had made his fortune in real estate and over the years Elizabeth had amassed a near fortune, a treasure chest of jewelry. She felt a woman could never have enough jewelry. It was a weakness, perhaps an obsession. In her later years, she had fits of memory loss and odd behavior. Sometimes she wore different earings on each ear. She was always misplacing her rings or bracelets and none of it was insured.

So it was to get away from the madding crowd of financial advisors that she had booked this cruise and to take her back a bit to her lost days of the theatre. She booked three suites on the ship to insure her privacy... an empty one on the left side, and another on her right side for the social host, and she took the middle one. Although the host was usually supplied by the cruise line, Mrs. Van had insisted on having her own exclusive companion. The cruise line consented and agreed to solicit for the right man.

The interview was a formality. Elizabeth Van was charming and reacted positively to John Solo. There was an immediate bond. The chemistry was right. They discussed her brief acting career and his frustrations in the theatre with its limited opportunities. He summed up his acting career as "being in the wrong place at the wrong time." He told her of the Shakespeare repertory group he was associated with in his younger days in Lenox, Massachusetts; that he had once played *Hamlet* in a college production; Anne Frank's father in a touring company, and as an understudy in an Off-Broadway production of *Inherit The Wind*. He added, "since the lead actor in the play was healthy, he went on for only one single performance as Clarence Darrow and it was only because the lead was too drunk to find the theatre. And just my luck," John continued, "none of the critics were there that night." Elizabeth got a laugh out of that one. They shook hands, signed all the papers and agreed that it would be a happy and relaxing cruise for all. John had enough time to buy some cruise clothes and pick up a volume of Shakespeare plays from Barnes and Noble.

Departure day arrived and as the ship slipped out of New York harbor, John popped open a bottle of champagne and they toasted, first to Elizabeth, then to John, and then to William Shakespeare. John assumed his duties with relish emoting on the high seas like he never did on any stage. His lungs were clear, his voice alternating appropriately with soft murmers or when needed as loud as a trumpet. He read to her every morning after breakfast on her balcony. At one point he went to the lower deck below her balcony and did his Romeo to her Juliet. The mornings were usually the lighter readings as in *As You Like It* and *All's Well That Ends Well*. Later it was *Hamlet, Macbeth*, and *King Lear*. Oddly she had requested Lady Macbeth's lines repeatedly. Elizabeth could be lightheaded one minute and serious the next. Sometimes she just closed her eyes as if John's words were like music. When not reading, he would walk with her around the deck and they would discuss the troubles with the theatre and the invasion of English productions on Broadway.

Mrs. Van usually napped in the late afternoon either on the deck or in her suite depending on the weather. It was during these times that John would discover Andrea, the room steward. She was Swedish, blonde, buxom, very quiet, even shy and she was assigned to Mrs. Van's three suites. There were always plenty of towels and amenities in the staterooms. She was always there if anything was needed. The beds were made promptly, the fruit bowl was delivered daily with a knife on a plate. If asked, Andrea would cut up the fruit. She offered extra pillows, blankets, coffee or breakfast in bed. She was cleaning girl, butler, valet. All that with a charming Scandinavian accent, and an effervescent smile at John. After two weeks at sea it was obvious that Andrea was smitten and began to swoon over John like a fan swoons over a matinee idol. John treated it like a joke and laughed it off. After four weeks, it became a ritual that as soon as Mrs. Van took her afternoon nap, John would seek out Andrea for a friendly chat which soon became a genuine flirtation. Simultaneously Elizabeth Van was undergoing a subtle emotional change that she couldn't quite understand.

On their strolls around the deck, John at first politely held her arm. At one point Mrs. Van took his hand and put it around her waist. John thought this was rather motherly inasmuch as Elizabeth was 20 years his senior. She seemed to elicit a joyful new intimacy. And with each new day she clasped his hands tighter, she laughed a little louder, and her eyes grew more sombre. It finally occurred to John that Elizabeth was becoming more possessive. She was drinking more now. Their champagne before dinner had increased from one glass as a toast to at least three or four. He had obviously awakened something in her that recalled more youthful days. It was kind of a late life attraction that she couldn't control.

John was performing in grand style recalling many of the roles he had done previously. On a day he was doing *Hamlet* on her veranda, he looked over the sea and then at her reciting those famous lines:

Doubt that the stars are fire;
Doubt that the sun doth move;
Doubt truth be a liar;

But never doubt I love

Elizabeth was almost transported spellbound by the sound of his voice. When he did *King Lear*, Elizabeth was mesmerized. To her they were John's words, not the Bard's:

> I love you more than words can wield the matter;
> Dearer than eye-sight space, and liberty;
> Beyond what can be valued, rich or rare;
> Beyond all manner of so much I love you.

After such words, John sensed that there had to be a cooling off period, and he often suggested that they go in for a glass of tea. To manage some variety in her shipboard life, Mrs. Van liked to go to the arts and crafts activity. The result of this activity was the making of two masks; the mask of comedy and the mask of tragedy. She placed it on her dressing table in the suite. Later she had pasted them on either side of an empty champagne bottle for display purposes. It reminded her of the theatre that she loved. Meanwhile John's relationship with Andrea continued, friendly and conversational on practically a daily basis in John's suite or whenever they met in the passageway outside the suites but only when Mrs. Van fell asleep on the deck.

So John Solo was soon sharing his attention and affections with a woman 20 years older than himself and one 20 years younger. He grew to admire Elizabeth Van and almost believed the lines he read to her from *Antony and Cleopatra*:

"Age cannot wither her, nor custom stale her infinite variety."

It mirrored his admiration for her and he was a bit astonished that he could actually feel so deeply for this person. Or maybe it was just what she represented and what was in it for him. He felt that as the cruise was in its final days, this was a curious but profitable gig. Possibly Elizabeth Van could be a valuable connection for some future acting work. This was foremost on his mind one day when Mrs. Van announced that she was very tired, had a light dinner, and retired early. John walked the deck alone, played black jack in the casino, thought he would go back to his suite, read, watch TV and call it a night.

It was about 11:30PM. He was groggy and almost asleep. All was still when there was a faint knock on his suite door, and then the door opened. Andrea walked in quietly wearing a loose robe and before John could speak, she had disrobed and climbed into bed with him. She did not speak. She didn't have to. John did not resist. He enveloped her bodily warmth.

That was the climax of a torrid affair that had been building like an ember that refused to be extinguished. Although this was a dangerous course for both of them, they both realized that the consequences could be serious. As for Mrs. Van, she certainly would not want to find her lovable social host hosting her room steward. John was walking a tightrope. It was a balancing act. Both women were obviously in love with him. While being attentive and intensely interested in Mrs. Van, he was enticed by Andrea's youth and beauty. She triggered in him desires that had been dormant for too long.

Mrs. Van was beginning to feel younger as if she was being courted. John had begun to tuck her into bed each night. She would say "Good night, sweet prince," and kiss him on the cheek or on the hand. He would respond with a flattering smile and leave never locking the door between their suites. And during the last week of the cruise Andrea would be waiting. This menage a trois continued until a few days before the trip terminated. The balancing act ended that night when Mrs. Van awoke and heard some rumbling. She opened the door to the suite on her left but found no one there. When she tried the door on the right and turned on her light, it was a sight that she never expected to see.

She hurried back to her suite while Andrea scurried out by the other door. Elizabeth was shaking. Her confusion led to anger and then to a jealous rage. John had dressed quickly then rushed into her suite... and rushed unknowingly into the plunging fruit knife that Elizabeth was holding in front of her. John dropped. Elizabeth fainted and had a stroke. All was quiet until Andrea slipped back into Mrs. Van's suite. She saw John lying on the floor lifeless and tried to awaken him thinking he was unconscious. Suddenly her hands were awash in his blood. Then instinctively she pulled the knife from his stomach and threw it on the floor.

When the authorities pieced things together, Andrea was arrested for the murder of John Solo.

Her fingerprints were on the knife and his blood was all over her robe. Mrs. Van remained in a coma. There were no other suspects or witnesses and the case was closed expeditiously without a major scandal. Nobody thought much of the fragment of the champagne bottle that had been knocked off the dresser resting near the body of John Solo. The fragment amidst the pool of blood was unmistakably the mask of tragedy that Elizabeth Van had made in her arts and crafts class.